LOUIS HÉBERT

and

MARIE ROLLET

Canada's Premier Pioneers

GEORGE & TERRY GOULET

FabJob Inc.

19 Horizon View Court,

Calgary, Alberta, T3Z 3M5

Printed in Canada

Cover photographs are of statues of Louis Hébert and Marie Rollet forming part of the Monument to them and Guillaume Couillard in Montmorency Park in Old Quebec City, Quebec.

Sculptor - Alfred Laliberté.

Cover photographer – Terry Goulet.

Library and Archives Canada Cataloguing in Publication Data

Goulet, George R. D. (George Richard Donald), 1933 -
   Louis Hébert and Marie Rollet: Canada's premier
pioneers/ George and Terry Goulet

Includes bibliography, references, and index.

ISBN-978-1-897286-15-9

        1. Hébert, Louis, 1575-1627. 2. Rollet, Marie, d. 1649.
3. Canada--History--To 1663 (New France).   4. Pioneers--Canada--
Biography. I. Goulet, Terry. II. Title.

FC332.1.H4G68 2007   971.01'10922   C2007-904227-9

... [Hébert's] agricultural proclivities make him by common consent the first true colonist of Acadia.

Charles W. Colby
Canadian Types of the Old Régime 1608-1698

.... Louis Hébert - first pharmacist in Canada, and probably the first to practice his profession on the North American continent.

George A. Bender
Great Moments in Pharmacy

.... here came Louis Hébert, an apothecary from Paris, who was later to be the first farmer at Quebec. Canadian agriculture and medicine may perhaps .... be said to have begun with him.

George W. Brown
Building the Canadian Nation

.... Marie Rollet was the first Frenchwoman to cultivate the soil of New France.

The Canadian Oxford Dictionary

.... she [Marie Rollet], and she alone, has to speak .... for the countless .... frontierswomen who shared with their husbands the hardships and dangers of the early life, and at the same time brought up those large families .... the pride of their nation....

Isabel Skelton
The Backwoodswoman

ACKNOWLEDGEMENTS

A number of years ago we were doing genealogical research for a family reunion when we discovered that the author George Goulet is a direct descendant of Louis Hébert and Marie Rollet. A relative, Bill Benoit, was then a genealogist at the Centre du Patrimoine in St. Boniface, Manitoba. With his assistance, we were able to obtain from La Société Historique de Saint-Boniface definitive proof of George's ancestry.

Once we became aware of this family connection with Louis Hébert and Marie Rollet, we soon realized what a remarkable role this duo played in the history of Canada. We then began the daunting task of researching the available information on this fascinating couple. The result of this research is this book that provides a factual account of Canada's first permanent pioneers, Louis Hébert and Marie Rollet.

Over the years, various projects interrupted this literary work. Consequently we are pleased to have finally brought it to fruition.

We wish to express our appreciation to various librarians, archivists and researchers in various libraries, museums and archives for their encouragement and assistance to us during our work on this book.

Our appreciation and thanks for their assistance and help is also extended to the staff of FabJob Inc. and in particular to Tag, Catherine and John.

We would also like to thank Laura and Mike de Jonge for their assistance; to Greg Head for the material and pictures he supplied to us; to Mike Harris for providing us with photographs; and to our son George Goulet and to Anson Ing for technical assistance.

Any errors herein are the responsibility of the authors.

This book is dedicated to our fabulous children and grandchildren who continue to give us love and support in all our endeavours.

Calgary, Alberta, 2007.

TABLE OF CONTENTS

Section D **The Family and Extended Family
of Louis Hébert and Marie Rollet**

DEFINITIONS

A number of terms used in the 1600s are not in common usage today. The following are definitions or descriptions of some of these words that appear herein.

apothecary – an historical name for a skilled practitioner who prepared and dispensed medicines. Formerly an apothecary also prescribed medication and performed the services of a physician. The medical profession took over these latter functions during the 1800s. This resulted in the principal role of an apothecary becoming that of a dispensing pharmacist and a professional who advises on the use of medicinal drugs. The current dictionary definition of apothecary is that of "pharmacist" or "druggist".

astrolabe – an instrument used to find the altitude of a star and other heavenly bodies and to assist in navigation until is was replaced by the sextant in the 18th century. It also had other uses such as surveying.

bustard – a long necked dry land bird normally associated with the Old World. In the context of North America, the bird referred to herein was probably a goose or wild turkey.

fief – usually heritable land held under the feudal system or in fee. It was normally granted in return for a form of duty, allegiance or service.

galette – a French term for a round flat cake and for a ship's biscuit.

matelot - a sailor or seaman (derived from the French). The word "Matelot" was part of the name of one of the fiefs of Louis Hébert.

mattock – a tool similar to a pickaxe with a flat adze-shaped blade used for digging up and cutting roots of trees. It could also be used as a hoe to break up the soil.

mortar and pestle – instruments used for mixing and grinding substances. The mortar is a hard heavy bowl and the pestle is the tool used for pounding and crushing ingredients in it. Historically, pharmacists used a mortar and pestle to prepare prescriptions. Consequently today they are the main symbol associated with pharmacy. It is interesting to note that the home in Paris where Louis Hébert was born and raised was named "Le Mortier d'Or" – The Golden Mortar.

pinnace – any of a kind of small boat used in conjunction with a large ship. It frequently had sails and was used as a tender to ferry people and goods to and from ships and for other activities.

shallop – any of various early small light open boats with oars, sails or both, from the late 16thcentury French word "chaloupe".

EXPLANATORY NOTE

Chapter Reference Sources

At the end of an applicable Chapter, a number of resource materials are listed under the heading "Chapter Reference Sources". Further information on these sources is provided in the "Bibliography". In the "Bibliography" the sources are arranged alphabetically under the last name of the applicable author or editor referred to in the "Chapter Reference Source".

Chapter I

PRELUDE

In the early 1600s Europe was alive with wars, diseases, poverty, and class and religious discrimination. Many saw it as a time to search the horizon for new challenges, new beginnings, and a better life.

Some saw their prospects and future in the New World across the Atlantic Ocean. In those days there were not the conveniences and comforts of today's travel. The journey by these early voyagers to their destination required travel in crowded and dirty quarters on a mast-rigged ship across treacherous waters.

Upon reaching their destination settlers would be faced with an untamed land to clear and conquer. In addition they would have to deal with unknown challenges, dangers and hostilities.

Their efforts would take courage, endurance and optimism. It is to these first permanent settlers that we need to give praise, for they contributed to making this country what it is today.

Early recorded history of frontier Canada is alive with an exceptional cast of colorful characters in a New World inhabited by unique indigenous peoples. The chronicles of this evolutionary period in Canadian history contain engaging tales of adventure and challenge.

Canadian annals are replete with struggles and achievements, hopes and disappointments, tragedies and triumphs. These ancestral tales demonstrate the courage, the perseverance, and the resourcefulness of these early actors on the Canadian scene.

This era does not want for romance and glory. It contains an historical and brilliant pageant of motley personalities, both native and European. These individuals include adventurers, explorers, traders, entrepreneurs, schemers, Indian chiefs, hunters, warriors, missionaries, coureurs-de-bois, voyageurs, pioneer settlers, intrepid women and country wives, all of whom contributed to the fabulous history and heritage of Canada.

Among the most remarkable of this cast of characters are Louis Hébert and his wife Marie Rollet. Some four centuries ago they left the cosmopolitan lifestyle of Paris, France to relocate to the undeveloped frontier of the New World.

In doing so they became the first colonial family to permanently settle in Canada. In their determination to make a home in this country, they undauntedly overcame disheartening barriers, handicaps, and adversities. They subdued the untamed land and laid the groundwork for the future development of the great nation of Canada.

They were the forerunners of the millions of men, women and children from all over the world who would immigrate to Canada to find a better life. The following is a factual account of the noteworthy lives and times of these two extraordinary trail-blazing pioneers.

SECTION A

EARLY EUROPEAN EXPLORATIONS

OF NORTH AND SOUTH AMERICA

**Viking Warrior
and Vessel**

by Charles W. Jefferys

Jacques Cartier's Ship

by Charles W. Jefferys

End of the 15th Century Ships

by Charles W. Jefferys

Chapter II

EARLIEST CONTACTS WITH THE NEW WORLD

Although Louis Hébert and his family were the first permanent colonial pioneers in Canada and he was the first apothecary to settle in the New World, a number of European explorers journeyed to North and South America many years and, in some instances, centuries before his arrival.

A brief background on some of these voyages starts with the legend of St. Brendan of County Kerry, Ireland. According to the ninth-century epic "The Navigation of St. Brendan", Brendan sailed from Ireland about the year 560 AD with a group of monks. The trip lasted some seven years.

On this legendary voyage in search of a promised land, they encountered some unusual experiences. Evil spirits threw balls of fire at them; they passed by huge buoyant crystal structures in the water; and a gigantic ocean creature lifted up their ship, before they finally reached a beautiful land with a great river cutting through it.

There is speculation that these incidents may have a more benign explanation. The fireballs flung at them by evil spirits may have been volcanic eruptions in Iceland; the huge buoyant structures in the water may have been icebergs; the gigantic ocean creature may have been an enormous whale; and maybe the beautiful land was Canada or some other part of North America.

In the 1970s British explorer Timothy Severin built a replica of the type of boat that may have been used by St. Brendan and his monks. With his crew he took a 50-day voyage, starting from Ireland and following almost the same route as the Vikings from the Faeroe Islands to Newfoundland. This modern-day trip succeeded in proving that such a craft was technically able to make this crossing.

Leaving this legend aside, it has been definitely established that the Vikings came to Canada around the last year of the 10th Century i.e. about 1000 AD. The Vikings were fearsome Scandinavian pirates who in the ninth, tenth and eleventh centuries sailed to various European lands where they raided, pillaged, and indiscriminately slaughtered.

The word 'viking' is from Icelandic 'vikingr', meaning a pirate. Viking has also been used as a verb to indicate piracy raids by Norsemen, inhabitants of ancient Scandinavia. Initially this was an area covering Norway, Denmark, and Sweden.

In the ninth century, besides forays into many European lands, these fierce northern marauders voyaged to the Faeroe Islands and Iceland and in the following century they traveled as far as Greenland.

Many of their exploits are known from sagas recorded in the Middle Ages, such as the Saga of Eric the Red and the Saga of the Greenlanders. Sagas are medieval Scandinavian prose narratives of battles, customs, legends, and notable Norse families.

Some believe they were founded on oral and written tradition, and are artistic constructs. They were written between the twelfth and the fourteenth centuries. The Icelandic Sagas record various voyages and events and some depict the epic adventures of Viking families in bloodthirsty detail.

Prominent Norsemen involved in their explorations included Eric the Red and his son Leif Ericsson. A recent five-volume translation of the Icelandic Sagas spells Ericsson's first name "Leifur".

Eric led an Icelandic flotilla to Greenland where he set up a colony in 985 or 986. A trader Bjarni Herjolfsson, in trying to meet up with Eric, failed to do so but on traveling east from southern Greenland he sighted what were likely Labrador and Newfoundland.

Eric's son Leif, who grew up in Greenland, subsequently sailed west of Greenland seeing many glaciers and the shores of Baffin Island, which was dubbed Helluland - the Land of Stone Slabs. Further along, Leif and his crew passed Labrador or Markland, the Land of Forests.

Sailing south of Markland, he landed and established a base at a site somewhere on the northeast coast of North America. He named this location Vinland, Land of Wine, because of the wild grapes growing in that area. Leif took timber and wine from Vinland to Greenland when he returned there.

Vinland's precise location is not known, but may have been in Newfoundland or the New England area of the United States, probably in the vicinity of the Gulf of St. Lawrence. Leif appears to have been the first European to walk on the North American mainland. However, after a short time, Leif and his entourage abandoned their camp and returned to Greenland.

Various Icelandic Sagas tell of these historic Viking voyages, but the only authenticated settlement of the Norse Vikings in North America is at L'Anse aux Meadows (a variation of French words meaning "Jellyfish Cove"). This site was established about 1000 AD at the northernmost tip of Newfoundland and was unearthed in the 1960s.

Archeological digs since then have found vestiges of a number of homes and work places, and various artifacts. In 1978 this major find was declared a United Nations World Heritage site. A re-enactment of the Viking voyage and landing at L'Anse aux Meadows, which included a 23 meter replica of the ship Islendigur, occurred in the year 2000.

L'Anse aux Meadows was a precursor of the wide-ranging role that Europeans were destined to play on the North American stage several centuries later.

In Viking folklore, the first European born in the New World was Snorri Thorfinnson, a member of Eric the Red's clan. Legend has it that he first came into this world at L'Anse aux Meadows, but subsequently his parents Thorfinnur Karlsefni and Gudrid Thorbjarnardottir returned to Iceland with Snorri.

There is a statue of Snorri and his mother in Iceland peering towards Newfoundland, evidence of the Icelandic belief in this saga.

Only a few years after Leif Ericsson returned home to Greenland, the Vikings gave up their interest in Vinland and any settlement efforts. Probable reasons for this withdrawal were the distances involved and their interests had turned to Europe where there were more resources available to them. As well the Sagas indicate that a brief time after Leif's departure, a group of Vikings who journeyed to the area encountered natives for the first time.

Although initial contact resulted in the bartering by the Vikings of metal instruments, tools, and cloth for furs from the natives, antagonisms soon developed. The Vikings called the natives "Skraelings" from the Norwegian word for "shrieker", which undoubtedly was an outward expression of the inner attitude of the natives to these Scandinavian interlopers on their lands.

Later in the 1000s, Norsemen went to France where they became known as Normans and the lands they settled were called Normandy. They eventually embraced Christianity.

Under William the Conqueror they sailed from Normandy, attacked Britain, defeated King Harold II at the Battle of Hastings in 1066 (known as the Norman Conquest), and William the Conqueror became the first Norman King of England.

Many years later a number of factors led to the exploration and eventually to the settlement of Canada, and in due course, to Louis Hébert's momentous immigration to the New World. The factors leading to those events are discussed in the following Chapter.

Chapter Reference Sources

- "Brendan, St." in *The Canadian Oxford Dictionary*, p. 173.
- "First Europeans, The" segment of *Origins, A History of Canada* - television documentary.
- *Globe and Mail, The* Newspaper, November 30, 2002, p. A-3.

- *Icelandic Sagas - The Complete Sagas of Iceland* editor Viðar Hreinsson, Vol. V.
- "L'Anse aux Meadows" in *The Canadian Encyclopedia*" p. 1296.
- *National Post*" Newspaper, July 29, 2000, p. A-4 .
- *Wilderness Women - Canada's forgotten history* by Jean Johnston, Chapter 1.

Chapter III

EARLY EXPLORATIONS IN THE NEW WORLD

Several centuries after the Vikings discontinued their travels to the New World, various elements contributed to the exploration and eventual settlement of Canada. Some of the influences that preceded this era included an unlikely medley of (i) the Crusades; (ii) Marco Polo; (iii) Oriental spices, silks and other treasures; (iv) fish and furs; (v) royal charters; and (vi) a Papal decree.

The Crusades were armed military missions by Christians to the Holy Land during the 11th to 13th Centuries. Their purpose was to recover by force from the Muslims this Land that abutted the eastern coast of the Mediterranean Sea.

The Crusaders did not wholly succeed in their objectives. For example in 1192 King Richard the Lion-Hearted, who led the Third Crusade, failed to recapture Jerusalem from the Muslims. The Crusaders were repulsed by Sultan Saladin, the legendary warrior, who had evicted the Crusaders from that city five years earlier.

However the ventures of the Crusaders to this land that is now modern-day Israel opened their eyes to the wondrous and opulent merchandise to be found in those lands. There were fine fabrics of satin and silk, aromatic spices, precious gems, and other desirable commodities. Many of these and other riches came to the Mid-East from the Orient by means of the Silk Road, a centuries-old caravan route connecting the Mid-East with central China. The Silk Road was so named because of the huge quantities of silk from China that were transported over it, usually by camels.

Muslim merchants traveled to those far-off areas of China, India, Indonesia, and other nearby countries returning home laden with Oriental goods. The Europeans, who had come to the Holy Land from afar to wage "holy wars", were fascinated by these exotic products, and wanted to obtain them.

Before long various riches of the Far East were making their way to Europe, including the major city states of what now is Italy. These cities developed into important trading areas for goods from the Far East.

The greatest of all medieval travelers was the Venetian Marco Polo. He further aroused the European desire for exotic merchandise from the Far East by writing about his lengthy journeys to and from Asia in the late 13th Century. He did so in his *Description of the World* (also known as *The Travels of Marco Polo*). When he was only seventeen years old he started out in 1272 with his father Nicola and his uncle Maffeo (Venetian traders) from Acre, now an Israeli seaport on the Mediterranean.

Their party traveled overland through Asia, crossed the Gobi Desert, went along the Silk Road to China and arrived at the court of the Mongolian Emperor of China, Kublai Khan, in 1275. They were impressed with what they saw and found.

Marco described Lin-an (today Hangshou) as the world's largest and most beautiful city. He and his group stayed in the Far East for many years and returned home in 1295 to Venice, a powerful and cultural city. Primarily traveling by sea they returned via India, Indonesia, and Persia. Marco's writings on this extended trip stimulated European interest in acquiring the fascinating riches of the Orient.

However this initial free-flow of Far East products to Europe along the Silk Road was not to last long. In the mid-fifteenth century, overland routes to and from the Orient became dangerous because of major political unrest in those far-off lands. As well, Muslims in the Middle East commenced obstructing passage by the Europeans to the Orient.

These problematic developments caused European traders and others to seek alternative means of passage to the Orient. At the time it was generally assumed that Asia was the land west of Europe across the Atlantic. The consequence was that in the latter part of the 15th century there was a dramatic explosion of exploration by various European countries seeking the Orient. Much of their efforts were directed westward across the Atlantic Ocean. This sequence of events resulted in the Europeans finding the lands that became known as North and South America.

Initially the great explorers of North America in this period were mainly Italian sailors from wealthy Italian ports such as Genoa and Venice. However, these intrepid Italian mariners frequently sailed on behalf of other nations - Christopher Columbus for Spain; John Cabot for England; Giovanni da Verrazano for France; and others.

As the ditty goes "In 1492, Columbus sailed the Ocean blue". The patrons of Christopher Columbus were King Ferdinand and Queen Isabella of Spain who financed his westward quest to find the Orient. He and his crew aboard three ships (the Nina, the Pinta, and the flagship Santa Maria) sailed west towards the setting sun across the Atlantic Ocean. They arrived in the New World in 1492 but did not actually reach the American mainland; rather they landed at several islands in the Caribbean Sea.

Mistakenly Columbus thought that he had reached the Indies, which were then considered to be India and the Malay Archipelago consisting of Indonesia, the Philippines and nearby regions. Consequently he designated the area as the Indies and as a result the indigenous people living there became known as Indians. Columbus never wavered in his belief that he had found India.

It has been generally considered that Columbus was the first European to "discover" America and make contact with the aboriginal peoples there. This is not true. It has been definitively established (as noted herein) that the Vikings were the first Europeans to arrive and encounter aboriginals.

In fact they established a settlement at L'Anse Aux Meadows in Newfoundland almost five hundred years before Columbus reached the shores of the Americas.

In 1992 many indigenous aboriginal people were offended by celebrations of the "discovery" of America by

Columbus 500 years earlier. Also if there is to be a day to honor the first visit by Europeans to the New World it should not be Columbus Day, but rather a day honoring the Viking explorers who, as noted, actually preceded Columbus to America by almost 500 years. In addition it should be noted that this "discovery" was only in the sense of the Europeans discovering something new to them as, of course, the aboriginal peoples had been in the Americas since time immemorial.

Furthermore there is the legend of St. Brendan that should be taken into consideration as a possible earlier European visit to the Americas.

Following the return of Columbus to Spain in 1492, Pope Alexander VI (supreme arbiter of Catholic countries) took a step that played a large role in the future of Canada. He arbitrarily directed the division of the New World between the Catholic rulers of Spain and Portugal. Pursuant to the Treaty of Tordesillas of June 7, 1494, a north-south line of partition was made some 1200 nautical miles west of the Cape Verde Islands.

This Treaty assigned the area east of that line to Portugal and the area west of the line to Spain. Portugal thought its share included the area now known as Brazil. This resulted in a heritage of Portuguese being the official language of Brazil, whereas Spanish dominates in many of the other South and Central American countries and Mexico.

One of the explorers to South America was the Italian Amerigo Vespucci who made two trips to the New World between 1499 and 1502 during which he explored the coastline of Brazil. In 1507 the German cosmographer Martin Waldseemmeller associated the name "America" with the Latin word of the first name of Vespucci, which was "Americus".

The name "America" might also have been derived from the Spanish "Amerrique", a name used by early explorers for the newly discovered lands. A mountain range in Nicaragua bears this Spanish name of "Amerrique".

Because of the Papal partition in 1494, Portugal also believed that Newfoundland and the nearby region were within its sphere of interest and several Portuguese navigators (such as Gaspar Corte-Real in 1500) explored there in the early 16th century. An abortive attempt at a settlement on Cape Breton Island in 1520 by Joao Alvares Fagundes failed and with it Portugal's activities in Canada died.

Subsequent to 1492, Columbus made several more voyages to the New World but didn't touch down on the mainland of South American until 1498. During this period of exploration, the distinction of being the first European to set foot in North America belongs to John Cabot.

He was an Italian explorer and navigator from Venice who was in the service of England under Henry VII (the first Tudor king). Cabot sailed west from Bristol, England aboard the ship Matthew to the New World in 1497. He reached North America, perhaps Newfoundland or Cape Breton Island, and claimed the land for England.

Cabot unsuccessfully sought to find the Northwest Passage, a water route through the northern part of America from the Atlantic Ocean to the Pacific Ocean. However, he did report on the extensive supply of fish in the area, which eventually led to numerous European fishing expeditions.

A re-enactment of the 1497 trip of Cabot occurred in 1997, five hundred years after the event, with a replica of the Matthew landing in Newfoundland. Cabot set out on another journey to the New World the following year, but he and his expedition disappeared and were never seen again.

However, within a year of the initial voyage of Cabot, a discovery was made which was to have a huge effect on both Western and Eastern history. Previously in 1488 a Portuguese navigator Bartholomeu Dias found that Africa could be rounded by sea from the Atlantic Ocean to the Indian Ocean.

His fellow countryman and navigator Vasco da Gama, in searching for the Orient, was the first European to sail to India from the Atlantic east around the Cape of Good Hope (which he did in 1497). From the Cape he traveled through the Indian Ocean and via the Arabian Sea to the Port of Calicut. On May 22, 1498 he arrived at this Port, where the calico fabric originated, and which is on the Malabar Coast of India. He reached this trade center by a sea route that bypassed the Muslim merchants of the Levant and the traders of Venice and Genoa.

As a result of the voyages by the early explorers to the New World it became evident that Atlantic Canada was teeming with fish. This was especially so off the Grand Banks (a huge shoal in the Atlantic Ocean off the southeast coast of Newfoundland).

Consequently many European fishermen from several countries including England, France, Spain, Portugal and Holland came to this area each summer during the 1500s. There they stocked up on the super-abundant supply of fish and then headed home to Europe with their catch before the winter set in.

However, further south two earth-shaking break-throughs occurred in 1513 and 1520 respectively. In the earlier year the Spanish explorer, Vasco Nunez de Balboa, found the Pacific Ocean by crossing the Isthmus of Panama overland.

After making his way through Panama, he gazed upon the beautiful Pacific Ocean "silent upon a peak in Darien" (words by the poet John Keats erroneously referring to Cortez rather than Balboa). This was an astonishing discovery because it meant that what Columbus had called India was actually another land of an unknown magnitude.

Subsequently in 1520 Ferdinand Magellan of Portugal, in the service of Spain, sailed west and rounded the South American continent by means of the strait now named after him. He reached the Philippines in 1521 where, unfortunately, he was killed. His remaining comrades continued west around Africa to Spain, arriving in 1522 and thus completing the first circumnavigation of the World.

In 1513 the Spanish explorer Juan Ponce de León landed on the coast of Florida (land of "abundant flowers") looking for the fabled Fountain of Youth.

Another noted Italian navigator was Giovanni da Verrazano who was retained by Frances I, the King of France. The King was spurred into action by the discoveries of Balboa and Magellan and wanted to participate in the riches of the Orient. As a result he commissioned Verrazano to cross the Atlantic to attempt to find a western sea-route to Asia.

Verrazano sailed his ship La Dauphine to the New World in 1524 arriving at what is now North Carolina. He thought he was near the Pacific Ocean, but that his route to it was blocked by land. Not having a clue as to how remote the Pacific actually was, he sailed north for some 3,000 kilometers along the eastern seaboard exploring that coast of North America.

He was so taken by the beauty of the Virginia coast he named the area "Arcadia", meaning a romantic or idyllic paradise. A few decades later the name Arcadia became Acadia, and it was the area of New Brunswick and Nova Scotia that subsequently became so identified.

Verrazano was the first European to locate Narragansett Bay (which extends into Rhode Island) and New York Harbor. His explorations confirmed that this area of land between the Atlantic and the Pacific Oceans was distinct, and not part of Asia.

Because of strife and struggles in which France was involved in Europe, King Francis I was too preoccupied to continue to devote his attention to the New World and it took France another decade, after hostilities had ceased, before it followed up on Verrazano's findings.

24

The next explorer for France in the New World was Jacques Cartier, a Frenchman, who led a transatlantic expedition from St. Malo in 1534. King Frances I charged him to look for gold and riches in the New World and to search for a route to Asia, i.e. to do what Verrazano had failed to do a decade earlier.

This 1534 voyage was the first of three expeditions by Cartier, and in it he traveled along the Newfoundland coast and then west down to the Strait of Belle Isle. He termed the southern coast of Labrador "the land that God gave to Cain". He located Prince Edward Island and sailed along the Gaspé Peninsula.

At the Bay of Gaspé, while searching for the elusive passage to Asia, he encountered natives for the first time. The Iroquois he chanced upon had come from their village Stadacona (now Quebec City). The natives referred to it as "Kanata", Iroquoian for a cluster of villages.

Cartier thought that they were referring to the entire region, not just their village, as "Kanata". Thus, it was he who gave us the name "Canada" for the entire country. On seeing the Iroquois who had come to fish, Cartier gave these natives knives, iron goods and a red cap for their chief in exchange for furs.

On land, Cartier and his men erected a large cross bearing the arms of France and the inscription "Vive le Roi de France", as a symbol of claiming this territory for France. Donnacona, the Iroquois chief, was unhappy with this cross but in due course accepted it, undoubtedly without recognizing its symbolic significance.

Cartier talked Donnacona into allowing him to take two sons of the Chief back to France with him. On his second trip to Canada in 1535, Donnacona's sons (who had become conversant in French) led him down the St. Lawrence River to Stadacona. Thinking the St. Lawrence River could be the Northwest Passage leading to Asia, Cartier left Stadacona after a few days with his crew. They headed west until they reached Hochelaga, another Iroquois village that he named Mont Real (now known as Montreal).

This trip alienated Cartier and Donnacona. Cartier remained in the area throughout the winter. Scurvy killed a number of his men until the Iroquois provided them with the remedy for this disease - the brew from the bark of the white cedar tree. This may have been the first use by Europeans of North American herbal medicine.

Cartier never did find the Northwest Passage. This achievement had to wait until the early 20th century when Roald Amundsen (a Norwegian polar explorer) successfully navigated this Passage aboard the Gjöa.

In 1536 Cartier treacherously abducted Donnacona, two of his sons, and several other Iroquois and sailed for France. He kidnapped them because the Chief had recently told him of a land of gold and riches - "the Kingdom of the Saguenay". Cartier wanted to take them to France so that they could personally inform the King of this Kingdom.

His intention was to induce the King to authorize a colonial settlement to search for these riches. This led to a third voyage by Cartier five years later that was intended to establish such a colony. In addition it was not Cartier who was to be in command but Jean-Francois de la Rocque, Sieur de Roberval. Cartier arrived in 1541, but relations with the natives soon deteriorated when the natives learned that Donnacona had died in France.

In 1542, believing that he had found gold and diamonds, Cartier decided to return to France with samples of his findings. On his way, he encountered Roberval in Newfoundland. Roberval ordered him to remain in Canada but Cartier surreptitiously left with his cargo, which proved to be worthless rock.

Roberval remained in Iroquois country until 1543, but became disheartened by the cold weather and the antagonistic Iroquois and abandoned the New World that year. His return to France ended attempts at exploration and colonization by France for over half a century. However, primarily because of John Cabot whose men had caught fish "with baskets", European countries became aware of the abundance of fish off Newfoundland.

Two Portuguese explorers Gaspar and Miguel Corte-Real, who journeyed in this region in 1501 and 1502 (including the Bay of Fundy), also spread word in Europe of the plentiful stock of fish in this area, particularly cod. In only a few years, a large number of fishing expeditions came to this area annually from such places as France, Brittany, England, Spain, Portugal and Holland.

Initially the Europeans preserved their fish catch by salting it when caught ("green fishing"), rather than drying it. However the English and Dutch lacked the necessary quantities of salt (produced by evaporation from seawater) required for extensive green fishing.

To overcome this problem, they developed the technique of "dry fishing". This was the method of drying the fish in the sun, which could only be done on a large scale on land. Eventually temporary summer villages were established in Newfoundland for dry fishing the catch prior to transporting it back to Europe.

Meanwhile the Basques, who were accomplished whalers in the Bay of Biscay, were primarily interested in hunting for whales especially in the Gulf of St. Lawrence. An interesting side note is that whales can still be found in the Bay of Fundy today.

In the summer of 2003 it was announced that shipping lanes in the Bay were being moved four miles east. The reason for so doing was to minimize the risk of ships colliding with the right whales which enter the Bay of Fundy each summer to feed.

In due course, France decided to pursue French settlement in the New World and a means of doing so was by grants of royal charters. French efforts to colonize Acadia and subsequently New France as well as the shift in priorities from fish to furs, is discussed in later Chapters. However, the following Chapters deal with an outline of Louis Hébert and his family and a brief background on Hébert's life prior to his first journey to Acadia in 1604.

Chapter Reference Sources

- *Canada - The Foundation of its Future* by Stephen Leacock, p. 23-24.
- "Cartier, Jacques" by Marcel Trudel, editor in chief James H. Marsh in the *Canadian Encyclopedia*, p. 406-07
- *Champlain: The Life of Fortitude* by Morris Bishop, p. 20.
- *Early Trading Companies of New France, The* by H. P. Biggar, p. 18-26.
- *Encyclopedia Britannica*, Vol. 9, p. 571-74; Vol 12, p. 328.
- *History of the Canadian People, A* by M. H. Long, Vol. 1, p. 210-11.
- "In Search of Asia" by Marcel Trudel in *Horizon Canada*, Vol. 1, p. 26-31.

SECTION B

LOUIS HEBERT

FIRST PIONEER FARMER, PHARMACIST, AND PERMANENT COLONIAL SETTLER IN CANADA

Stamp Honoring Louis Hébert

©Canada Post Corporation

Home of Louis Hébert and Marie Rollet on the cliff above
L'Habitation at Quebec.

Chapter IV

A *RARA AVIS* - A REMARKABLE PERSON

While not well known in the annals of Canada, the saga of Louis Hébert is remarkable and stirring. Hébert was a "*rara avis*", a resolute and brave visionary who was a pioneer in sowing the seeds of the early development of Canada.

Although some sources mention that his first trip was in 1606, a number of other resource materials indicate that Louis Hébert made his first journey to the New World in 1604. In either case, he arrived before Jamestown was established in Virginia in 1607, and before the Pilgrims landed at Plymouth Rock, Massachusetts in 1620.

Assuming that the 1604 sources are correct, his first journey to Acadia was with the expedition of Pierre Du Gua, Sieur de Monts. Jean de Biencourt, Sieur de Poutrincourt (Hébert's first cousin's husband) also accompanied this venture. Hébert came to Acadia three times between 1604 and 1613. He and his wife Marie Rollet were living in Port Royal, Acadia in 1613 when the English overthrew and destroyed the French settlement there. Subsequently he and his family settled in Quebec City in 1617 and he later received title to his lands there in the 1620s. Other members of the extended Hébert family were also shining lights in early Canada.

At the time of the arrival of the Hébert family in Quebec there were three European families employed with the fur trading company in Canada. However Louis Hébert's wife Marie Rollet was the first European woman to come to Canada with her family to permanently settle and farm the land. *The Canadian Oxford Dictionary* states:

> .... she was the first Frenchwoman to cultivate the soil of New France.

Marie Rollet had a great affection for the native children and was particularly concerned about and took an active interest in their education. She also demonstrated great fortitude in remaining in Canada with her children, son-in-law Guillaume Couillard, and grandchildren after the English conquered Quebec, and transported Champlain and most of the other Frenchmen back to Europe in 1629.

Guillaume Couillard, who married Louis Hébert and Marie Rollet's daughter Guillemette in Quebec in 1621, was the first person in Canada to use a plow, doing so the year after Hébert's death. Subsequently King Louis XIV made Couillard a seigneur. There are myriad descendants of Guillaume and his wife Guillemette in Canada today.

Numerous Quebec old-time families trace their ancestry directly to them and, of course, to Louis Hébert and Marie Rollet. Many Western Canadian families (including the authors' grandchildren who are fourteenth generation Canadians) are also direct descendants of Louis Hébert and Marie Rollet.

Guillemette Couillard (nee Hébert), the daughter of Louis and Marie, inherited much of the land that her parents and husband had owned in Quebec. Prior to her husband Guillaume's death, they had donated in the 1650s various lands to the Roman Catholic Church including land for the first hospital in Canada, the Hôtel-Dieu.

After her husband's death, Guillemette sold land to the Church including property for the petit seminaire (a small seminary). Part of the Séminaire de Quebec became Laval University in the 19th century. Another landmark that is today situated on these lands in the heart of Old Quebec is Notre Dame Basilica.

Although Hébert has not been generally acclaimed in Canada in a manner befitting his distinguished role in Canadian history, he has not been totally ignored, particularly in Quebec.

There is a huge monument in the heart of Old Quebec City in which a larger-than-life statue of Hébert has been placed on a high pedestal in Montmorency Park. This statue originally stood on the grounds of the Quebec City Hall prior to being relocated to its present site in the Park. This statue depicts Hébert proudly standing on the soil of his adopted homeland while holding high in the air a sheaf of Canadian wheat in one hand and a sickle in the other.

An English translation of the French inscription on this splendid monument to the first European settlers in Canada reads.

LOUIS HÉBERT

Louis Hébert, apothecary from Paris, explored Acadia in 1604 with Sirs de Monts and de Poutrincourt, and he resided there from 1606 to 1613. He settled in Quebec in 1617 with his family, and died January 25, 1627.

On one side of the extended base of the pedestal is a statue of his son-in-law Guillaume Couillard with his hand on a plow. Engraved under his name are the years "1613-1663", the former being the year he first arrived in Quebec as an employee to work at the fur-trading fort and the latter being the year of his death at Quebec.

Statues of Hébert's wife Marie Rollet and their three children are on the other side of the base. An English translation of the French engraving on the base reads: "Marie Rollet and her children. 1617-1649", the respective years in which she arrived in Quebec and when she died there.

In 1912 Abbé Azarie Couillard Després, a direct descendent of Hébert, wrote a biography in French entitled *Louis Hébert, Premier Colon Canadien et sa Famille* (*Louis Hébert, First Canadian Settler and his Family*). This book contains intermittent high-flown expressions of praise and flowery language concerning this notable ancestor of Després.

An abbreviated account (of less than 20 pages) about Hébert was written by Rosemary Neering for youthful readers; it was published in 1990.

Richard Boutet, a Quebec producer, made a film synthesizing some four centuries of Quebec history. It includes an outline of the legacy of Louis Hébert.

In 1966 Parke, Davis & Company published the book *Great Moments in Pharmacy* with stories written by George A. Bender. This book deals with highlights of pharmacy from before the dawn of history and thereafter - in Ancient Babylonia, Ancient China, etc. It provides information on prominent historic apothecaries and pharmacists such as Galen, Avicenna, Damian, and others. There is a chapter on Louis Hébert that commences:

> Nowhere is the intrepid spirit of self-sacrifice and service to fellowmen which has marked the lives of many pharmaceutical pioneers better exemplified than in the life of Louis Hébert - first pharmacist in Canada, and probably the first to practice his profession on the North American continent.

This section on Hébert is accompanied by a painting by Robert Thom. It depicts a creative illustration of Hébert inspecting drug plants proffered to him by a friendly Micmac Indian on the shores of Port Royal in Acadia. This work of art is a symbol of the friendly attitude of Hébert towards the natives, and the open and inquiring mind he possessed.

Hébert is frequently mentioned in many books and articles dealing with the history of Canada. For example, McGill University history professor Charles W. Colby in his biography of Samuel Champlain titled *The Founder of New France: a Chronicle of Champlain* devoted several paragraphs to Hébert calling him "the first real colonist" in Quebec. Colby is more elaborate in his book *Canadian Types of the Old Régime 1608-1698*, devoting a chapter to Hébert titled "The Colonist – Hébert". The following are several quotes from that book:

> Hebert's labours are so meritorious that posterity should preserve with pious care whatever is known about him.

> ... [Hébert's] agricultural proclivities make him by common consent the first true colonist of Acadia.

> Hebert deserves all the praise which belongs to a brave, a persevering, and a useful man .... in selecting an individual colonist who shall prefigure the whole class, one finds that his claims are paramount.

Most other sources in referring to Hébert usually do so in a brief manner. Thomas B. Costain in his book *The White and the Gold: The French Regime in Canada* wrote several pages about Hébert. Costain stated that Hébert is "rightly called the first Canadian settler".

In the 1931 article titled "On Apothecaries, Including Louis Hébert", the physician W. H. Hattie wrote:

> At Port Royal he [Hébert] was known as the herb gatherer, and his zeal for gardening so infected others that he is known as Canada's first agriculturist .... he was a man of parts and refinement.... There he devoted himself to agriculture and other community interests, in recognition of which he was styled the Patriarch of New France.

The Canadian Oxford Dictionary has a few lines on Hébert indicating that he first came to New France in 1604, without specifying that it was Acadia.

The Dictionary of Canadian Biography has a write-up on Hébert. It covers about a page and one-half and refers to him as the:

> .... first Canadian settler to support himself from the soil.

Samuel E. Morison, a Harvard University history professor, in his biography *Samuel de Champlain* writes that Louis Hébert was "one of the most important founders of Canada after Champlain".

The Canadian Encyclopedia has a brief write-up on our first Canadian settler as well, mentioning that he came to Canada three times between 1604 and 1613 and subsequently settled in Quebec City.

In the Preface to his *Dictionnaire Généalogique des Familles Canadiennes* written in 1871, Abbé Cyprien Tanguay wrote:

> Hébert, you were the first to draw your happiness, your glory, and all your blessings from the Canadian soil.
>
> Couillard, a noble and dignified recruit like you, enriched it by bringing the plough to these shores. To these first colonists honour, one hundred times honour.

In the text, Tanguay added further information about Louis Hébert and his family.

In addition to these references to Hébert, there are federal and provincial parliamentary constituencies in Quebec bearing the name Louis Hébert.

In 1985 the Canadian Government issued a thirty-four cent stamp memorializing the contributions of Louis Hébert to Canada. The artistic rendition for this stamp has the words "Louis Hébert, apothicaire/apothecary" and it depicts him with a mortar and pestle, with a scythe, and with herbs and plants.

At the home in Paris where Hébert was born and grew up there is a plaque affixed to the outside wall reading as follows:

ICI NAQUIT EN 1575

LOUIS HÉBERT

1st COLON EN ACADIE

ET A QUEBEC

The English translation is:

HERE WAS BORN in 1575

LOUS HÉBERT

1st COLONIST IN ACADIA

AND AT QUEBEC.

The Hébert home in Paris was known as the Mortier d'Or [Golden Mortar] and still exists today at 129 rue Saint-Honoré, less than two blocks from the Louvre Art Museum. A current photo of the Mortier d'Or together with a photo of the plaque on the home, are found in Appendix "B" of this book.

Today, in the heart of old Quebec City there are streets bearing the surnames of the Hébert and Couillard families, and there is a small European-style hotel named Hotel Marie-Rollet.

Louis Hébert and Marie Rollet were a valiant and adventurous duo. They were, in many respects, the premier Canadian couple.

If their impressive accomplishments had taken place in an American context, they would undoubtedly be considered American folk heroes, and the names and contributions of these inspiring personalities and their family would be widely admired and celebrated in the United States.

If heroes are persons distinguished by their outstanding achievements, courage, and noble qualities, then Louis Hébert and his wife Marie Rollet both deserve to be recognized and honored as heroes throughout the nation for their courageous and noteworthy contributions to Canada.

Chapter Reference Sources

- *Canadian Types of the Old Regime: 1608-1698* by Charles W. Colby, ch. IV.
- *Dictionnaire Généalogique des Familles Canadiennes* by Abbé Cyprien Tanguay, Vol. 1, Preface; p. 301.
- *Founder of New France: a Chronicle of Champlain, The* by Charles W. Colby, p. 67, 80-81.
- *Great Moments in Pharmacy* by George A. Bender, p. 72.
- "Hébert, Louis" in the *Canadian Encyclopedia* by Jacques Bernier, edited by James H. Marsh, p. 1060.
- "Hébert, Louis" in *The Canadian Oxford Dictionary,* p. 652.
- "Hébert, Louis" in the *Dictionary of Canadian Biography,* Vol. I, p. 367-68.
- *Louis Hébert: Premier Colon Canadien et sa Famille* by Abbé Azarie Couillard Després, *passim.*
- "On Apothecaries, Including Louis Hebert" by W. H. Hattie in *The Canadian Medical Association Journal,* January 1931, p. 120-23.
- *Samuel de Champlain - Father of New France* by Samuel Eliot Morison, p. 189.

Chapter V

LOUIS HÉBERT AND HIS FAMILY

Louis Hébert was born in Paris, France in 1575. His father was Nicolas Hébert, and his mother was Jacqueline Pajot. Louis was born in his parent's home, Le Mortier d'Or (Golden Mortar), situated at 129 rue Saint-Honoré. The term "Mortar" is appropriate as it refers to the bowl in which an apothecary or pharmacist grinds or pounds ingredients with a pestle. The house was l-shaped with part of it facing onto rue des Poulies. It is less than two blocks from the Louvre.

The Louvre, situated on rue de Rivoli, was an ancient royal palace next to the Seine River. It was converted into an art museum in the 18th century. As noted, Le Mortier d'Or exists to this day, and there is plaque affixed to it identifying it as the birthplace of Louis Hébert in 1575. A current photo of the house, as well as a photo of the plaque that provides a monument to Louis Hébert, can be found in Appendix "B" of this book.

Nicolas Hébert, the father of Louis, was an apothecary and physician at the court of Queen Catherine de Medici. Her husband King Henry II ruled France from 1547 to 1559. In 1560, after the death of her son François II (who was married to Mary, Queen of Scots), Catherine ruled France as regent during the minority of her second son Charles IX.

The mother of Louis Hebert, Jacqueline Pajot, was the aunt of Claude Pajot who was married to Jean de Biencourt de Poutrincourt, Baron de Saint-Just. Claude Pajot was Louis Hébert's first cousin and her marriage to Poutrincourt was to lead directly to Hébert's ventures, and the eventual permanent settlement of Hébert and his family, in the New World.

Louis followed in his father's footsteps and became an apothecary. However, his subsequent actions made clear that he not only yearned for greater freedom, but also to own his own land where he could grow herbs and crops. It was clear that he possessed an adventurous spirit.

Louis Hébert married Marie Rollet in Paris about 1601. They had three children, a son Guillaume and two daughters Anne and Guillemette. Their daughter Anne married Étienne Jonquest within a year after the Hébert's arrival in New France. This was the first formal marriage of Europeans in Quebec. She died without issue within a year of her marriage.

Their son Guillaume was wed to Hélène Desportes at Quebec and had only one child Joseph. Joseph's only son (also Joseph) died in infancy. The other daughter of Louis and Marie, Guillemette, had 10 children with her husband Guillaume Couillard whom she married on August 26, 1621 in L'Habitation in Quebec. Hers is the first marriage shown in the Registers of the Parish of Notre Dame.

One of the daughters of Guillaume Couillard and Guillemette Hébert was Elizabeth Couillard who was born in Quebec on February 9, 1631 when it was under the rule of England. It is through Elizabeth that the grandchildren of the authors of this book trace their direct lineage to Louis Hébert and Marie Rollet.

Louis Hébert's only great grandson bearing the last name Hébert died in early childhood; consequently there are no direct descendants of Louis Hébert bearing his surname. There is a Hébert Family Reunion at the World Congress of Acadians held about every five years (e.g. in New Brunswick in 1994 and in Louisiana in 1998). Those involved in these Reunions acknowledge that they trace their surname through other Héberts who immigrated to North America after Louis Hébert and Marie Rollet's arrival in Canada.

Through their daughter Guillemette and her husband Guillaume Couillard, there are numerous descendants of Louis Hébert and Marie Rollet living in Canada today.

Chapter Reference Sources

- "Hébert, Louis" by Ethel M. G. Bennett in *Dictionary of Canadian Biography*, Vol. I, p. 367-368.
- *Louis Hébert - Premier Colon Canadien et sa Famille* by Abbé Azarie Couillard Després, p. 55; 64-65; 104-05.
- "Recherches sur Louis Hébert et sa famille" in *Mémoires de la Sociètè Génealoquie Canadienne-Français* by M. Jurgens, VIII-No. 1, January, 1957, p. 107*et seq*; Vol. VIII-No. 3, July, 1957, p. 135 *et seq.*

Chapter VI

EARLY FRENCH SETTLEMENT IN THE NEW WORLD

As noted previously, since the early 1500s many European countries had been aware of the abundant fish stocks in the waters off the coast of Newfoundland. English, Basque, Breton, Norman and other European fishermen traveled in fleets to the Grand Banks as early as the first decade of that century. Each spring and summer they caught cod, turbot, and other species of fish and returned home to Europe with their catch in the fall.

By the middle of the 16th century, many of them were drying their fish on the shores of Newfoundland where they set up summer settlements for this purpose. After the fishing season ended and before winter set in, they loaded their cargo for the transatlantic trip back to Europe.

The fish-drying on land led to interaction with the native inhabitants who brought furs to trade for metal knives, kettles, pots and pans, and other European goods previously unknown to them. Originally only a sideline, the acquisition of furs eventually resulted in the fur trade surpassing fish in the priorities of the ship-owners and the European merchants that they traded with.

The prime reason for this eclipse was that the traditional sources of fur-bearing animals, Scandinavia, Northern Russia and Siberia, had been drastically depleted by over-hunting. At that time clothing (coats, muffs, hats, and other items) made from the pelts of foxes, beavers, ermines, sables, and other animals was reserved for the affluent upper-class, rich merchants and the aristocracy of Europe.

As well, the high-crown broad-brim felt hat made from fur, particularly beaver pelts, had become highly fashionable and a mark of one's status in society. This hat continued to be in demand in the last decades of the 16th century, throughout the 17th century, and for many years thereafter.

This combination of factors led merchants to look to the northern areas of the New World to meet the demand for furs. Canadian beaver pelts were of exceptional quality, thus making them especially desirable for the production of these hats.

By the middle of the 16th century, many Europeans (who had originally come to fish but had developed a profitable sideline in furs) were meeting yearly with the natives at Tadoussac where furs were bartered for European goods.

The native village of Tadoussac was at the confluence of the Saguenay and St. Lawrence Rivers, some 200 kilometers northeast of what is now Quebec City. Before the end of that century European fur traders, not fishermen, were journeying further down the St. Lawrence River. They did so to acquire pelts at the native village of Hochelaga, at the site where Montreal is now located.

This decision to actively promote the fur trade in Canada was to have a significant effect on Canadian history for centuries to come. About the time that the change of emphasis from fish to furs was occurring, Henry of Navarre (the founder of the Bourbon Dynasty) became King of France in 1589 under the name of Henry IV.

The acknowledged leader of the Huguenots Henry converted to Catholicism, thereby ending the religious civil wars. On March 22, 1594, amidst the cheers of the populace he went to hear the *Te Deum* at Notre Dame and is reputed to have said, "Paris is well worth a Mass".

It wasn't many years after his coronation that Henry IV decided to pursue French settlement in the New World, initially at Acadia. The principle purpose for doing so was to protect France's claim to the lands and their resources, particularly furs and the fur trade. Other considerations included:

- a desire for the discovery of gold and other minerals;

- an ambition to explore for regions as yet unknown;

- a wish to convert the natives (whom Henry called "barbarous atheists") to Christianity, and

- as always to seek out the elusive route to the riches of the Orient.

To save putting up royal funds for these purposes, Henry bestowed a fur-trading monopoly by the issuance of a Royal Patent. On November 8, 1603, the King issued a patent to Pierre du Gua, Sieur de Monts (a Gentleman Ordinary of the King's Chamber). De Monts was a French Huguenot born about 1558 who became a trader, explorer and colonizer.

He had first sailed to Quebec in the year 1600 as a curious observer with the Pierre Chauvin expedition. Chauvin was a merchant ship owner from Honfleur, whose second-in-command was François du Pontgravé of St. Malo.

In the Royal Patent of 1603 for Acadia, de Monts was appointed Lieutenant General to represent the King and do whatever was required for:

> .... the conquest, peopling, inhabiting, and preservation of the said land of La Cadie .... under our [the King's] name and authority.

This mandate required de Monts to colonize Acadia. It also required him to work for the conversion of the local natives to the Christian religion, as well as to search for minerals and to populate, to fertilize and:

> .... to make the said lands to be inhabited as speedily, carefully and skillfully as time, places and commodities may permit..

De Monts was granted exclusive trading privileges in Acadia with the right to take and retain "what you will". Acadia covered lands that primarily included the areas of present-day Nova Scotia, New Brunswick and parts of Maine.

De Monts had previously traveled to Acadia and other areas of New France as indicated by the Royal Patent itself. Immediately after he received the Patent, de Monts set to work to organize a voyage to these lands. One of his steps was to ask the French nobleman Jean de Biencourt, Sieur de Poutrincourt of Picardy, to join him in the Acadian adventure, and Poutrincourt agreed to do so.

Others who sailed with them were Louis Hébert (a Parisian apothecary) and Samuel Champlain (a cartographer who several years later on the instructions of de Monts established a fur-trading fort at what is now Quebec City).

The two ships of de Monts' expedition left France separately on March 7, 1604 and arrived in Acadia in May of that same year. A decision was made to establish a settlement on St. Croix Island in the southwest area of the Bay of Fundy, close by modern day New Brunswick.

This small island is situated in the St. Croix River in Maine. It is located just inside the United States boundary dividing that State from the Province of New Brunswick in Canada. Today it is an historic site under shared Canadian and American administration.

En route (while anchored at a harbor in what is now Nova Scotia) an amusing incident occurred on May 13, 1604. A sheep jumped overboard and drowned, but was recovered from the water and subsequently eaten. De Monts promptly gave this location the French name Port-au-Mouton (literally translated Port of the Sheep), and it bears that name to this day.

Not far away De Monts encountered a Frenchman Captain Rossignol in the act of acquiring fur pelts from the natives. This was a breach of de Monts' trading monopoly and he had Rossignol's ship seized. The provisions of the confiscated ship were a godsend as the food supplies of the de Monts expedition were rapidly being depleted.

The other ship in de Monts' venture under the command of François du Pontgravé had left France a few days after de Monts. However that ship had failed to meet up with the de Monts party in Acadia. Pontgravé's crew found some Basque ships trading with the natives at a port (now Louisbourg) on Cape Breton Island, and confiscated their goods.

After landing on the island of St. Croix, de Monts' men set about constructing various buildings. These included lodgings, a blacksmith shop, a cookhouse, a bakery, a storehouse and a palisade. Gardens were also planted.

As winter came on with its frigid temperatures, it was soon realized that the island was not suitable for long-term settlement. Its drawbacks included a lack of fresh water, separation from the mainland, poor soil for farming, and a harsh climate. However it was too late to relocate to a more favorable site. Consequently they had no choice but to pass their first winter at the St. Croix location.

Not only was the winter severe but many men died of scurvy, while dozens of others were sorely afflicted with this condition. Scurvy is a disease resulting from a deficiency of Vitamin C in the body.

Symptoms include bleeding from the mucous membranes, swollen bleeding gums, anemia, and weakness. Francis Parkman in his book *Pioneers of France in the New World* states:

> Soon the scurvy broke out, and raged with a fearful malignity. Of the seventy-nine, thirty-five died before spring, and many more were brought to the verge of death. In vain they sought that marvelous tree that had relieved the followers of Cartier. Their little cemetery was peopled with nearly half their number, and the rest bloated and disfigured with the relentless malady, thought more of escaping from their woes than of building up a transatlantic empire.

Unfortunately the natives in the area were unfamiliar with the tree-bark remedy provided by the Iroquois to Jacques Cartier some seventy years earlier.

In her *History of Medicine in the Province of Quebec*, Maude Abbott wrote of the attempts that were made by de Monts' party to find the cause of the scurvy

> .... by a post-mortem examination of those who had succumbed. In Acadia during the terrible wrath of 1604-

05 at Ile St. Croix, this duty had been carried out by Louis Hébert, surgeon-apothecary of the company.

In his book, Abbé Després wrote that Louis Hébert studied the symptoms of scurvy and attempted to stop its progress but he was unable to do so.

When the spring of 1605 came, a decision was made to abandon the settlement at St. Croix and find a more suitable and temperate site. A more appropriate location with brooks, valleys, lakes, and mountains was found on the opposite side of the Bay of Fundy on the north shore of the Annapolis Basin, close to the mouth of the Annapolis River. This land was named Port Royal.

Buildings on St. Croix Island were dismantled and their planks, timbers, and materials transported across the Bay in pinnaces (small boats of larger ships) and reassembled at a site in Port Royal in the summer of 1605. The settlement was called L'Habitation; it was built nearby present-day Annapolis Royal, Nova Scotia.

On the request of de Monts, Poutrincourt had returned to France in the fall of 1604 with a large quantity of furs, including the furs that had been confiscated from the illegal traders. However, Poutrincourt had earlier sought from de Monts the beautiful lands around Port Royal that had been sighted before the expedition settled on St. Croix Island; and de Monts had bestowed these lands on him with a condition that Poutrincourt colonize it.

This was quite agreeable to Poutrincourt. He was enchanted with the area and wished to live and "settle with his family and fortune there" according to Marc Lescarbot, an author who wrote about his 1606-07 experiences in Acadia.

One may conclude that Louis Hébert returned with Poutrincourt to France from Acadia in the fall of 1604. This would be consistent with resource materials that indicate that Hébert had arrived in Acadia that year. All sources state that in 1606 Hébert accompanied Poutrincourt on his return to Port Royal from France. In light of events in an ensuing chapter, one may also conjecture that Hébert's visit to Acadia in 1604 was to look into this area as a possible future home.

Chapter Reference Sources

- "Acadia, History of" in the *The Canadian Encyclopedia*, editor in chief James H. Marsh, p. 11.
- *Calgary Herald* Newspaper, July 20, 2003, p. A 1-2.
- *History of Medicine in the Province of Quebec* by Maude Abbott, p. 13.
- *Louis Hébert* by Julia Jarvis, p. 2.
- *Louis Hébert - Premier Colon Canadien et sa Famille* by Abbé Azarie Couillard Després, p. 17 *et seq.*
- *Nova Francia - A Description of Acadia, 1606* by Marc Lescarbot, translation by P. Erondelle, p. 4; 5; 7-10; 13; 32; 34; 61; 92, note 5 p. 331.
- "Partners in Trade" segment of *Origins, A History of Canada.*
- *Pioneers of France in the New World* by Francis Parkman, Vol. Two, ch. III.
- *Samuel de Champlain - Father of New France* by Samuel Eliot Morison, p. 36-37; 92.

Chapter VII

LOUIS HÉBERT'S LIFE IN ACADIA

As noted earlier, Poutrincourt was married to Louis Hébert's first cousin Claude Pajot. It was undoubtedly this family relationship with Poutrincourt that led to Hébert's presence on the 1604 expedition of de Monts to Acadia. Poutrincourt was then about 46 years old while Hébert was 28 years of age.

To put the period of time into perspective, Louis Hébert first came to Acadia only a year after the death of Queen Elizabeth I, and while William Shakespeare was at the height of his career writing English plays and literature.

Later that year de Monts sent Poutrincourt, along with Hébert, back to France with the furs seized from the two ships. Poutrincourt and Hébert returned to Port Royal from France on the ship Jonas in 1606. Also on this ship was Marc Lescarbot, a Parisian lawyer and author whom Poutrincourt had invited to this new land.

Although Lescarbot stayed for only one year, he set forth his Acadian experiences as well as his thoughts in a fascinating record titled *Histoire de la Nouvelle France*. A translation of part of his book is found in his *Nova Francia, a Description of Acadia, 1606*.

In this work Lescarbot wrote of Port Royal:

This port is environed with mountains on the North side; towards the South are small hills, which (with the said mountains) do pour out a thousand brooks, which makes that place more pleasant than any other place in the world; there are very fair water falls, suitable to make mills of all sorts. At the East is a river between the said mountains and hills, in which the ships may sail fifteen leagues and more, and in all this distance there is nothing on both sides of the river except fair meadows.

In *Canada - the Foundation of its Future*, the author Stephen Leacock wrote that Port Royal was:

.... a beautiful settlement in a great quadrangle of spacious houses of fragrant logs - kitchens, offices and smoking chimneys, snug as comfort itself - embowered with gardens, gorged with fruit and fish, fowl and game.

Incidentally, while Stephen Leacock is well known for his humorous writings (such as the 1912 work "Sunshine Sketches of a Little Town"), he was a professor at McGill University and a political economist and historian who wrote scholarly books in that genre.

In addition to the buildings mentioned by Leacock, other buildings at L'Habitation at Port Royal included lodgings, a dining hall, storehouses, a forge, an oven, and an arched gateway with a short path leading to the water. Four cannons were mounted on a bastion.

Lescarbot wrote that he went to Port Royal not so much out of a desire to see the new country but "to give an eye judgment of the land". With his classical education and entertaining writing style, Lescarbot sprinkled his work of 1609 with both factual information and personal anecdotes. These included the foretelling of storms by porpoises, how gusts of wind are formed, the sounds of the voices of seals being like that of owls, a description of a beaver, and other fascinating matters.

A map of Port Royal in Lescarbot's book (reproduced in Appendix "C" of this book) identifies a nearby river as the Hébert River, obviously named after Louis Hébert. However, a subsequent English corruption of this French surname resulted in its current name of Bear River and the naming of a nearby island as Bear Island. The distortion undoubtedly is due to the last syllable of Hébert's name being pronounced with a French accent as "bear".

Lescarbot's book *Nova Francia – A Description of Acadia, 1606* was published not long after his return to France. This resulted in a falling out between Lescarbot and Champlain. Champlain felt that he should have been the first chronicler to describe events in Acadia.

In comparison with Champlain's rather pedestrian prose, Lescarbot with his classical training wrote in a highly entertaining style that appealed to his readers. This dispute degenerated into childish accusations by both parties.   Champlain claimed that Lescarbot had been infested with fleas at an Indian conclave at St. Croix, while Lescarbot accused Champlain of being a believer in the legendary Micmac forest monster, the "Gougou".

Champlain described what the natives told him about Gougou. They said that it lived on an island, had the form of a hideous woman, made horrible noises, and was so huge that the tops of the masts of the French ships would not reach its waist.

The natives captured by Gougou were placed in its great pocket, large enough to put a vessel in, and later it ate them. Champlain wrote:

> And what makes me believe what they say is the fact that all the savages in general fear it .... but I hold that this is the dwelling-place of some devil that torments them in the manner described.

One of Champlain's biographers Samuel E. Morison states that Lescarbot:

> .... is an indispensable source for Champlain's Acadian phase.

According to another writer and translator William F. Ganong (as quoted in S. E. Morison's book) Champlain's annoyance with Lescarbot was likely due to:

> .... the antagonism between the man of action and the man of letters...

When Poutrincourt, Hébert, Champlain and others were off exploring the New England coastline in the fall of 1606, Lescarbot was left in charge of Port Royal. During their absence Lescarbot, who was also a playwright, conceived the idea of writing and presenting a play to welcome the explorers back to Port Royal.

The first play ever written and performed in Canada and, likely, in North America was his *Le Théâtre de Neptune*.   Written in French rhymes, it was staged on November 16, 1606 at Port Royal for the inhabitants and the natives including the elderly native Chief Membertou, the sagamore (supreme chief) of the Souriquois.

This performance was followed by a sumptuous banquet accompanied by flagons of wine. Some 400 years later, on November 14, 2006, Lescarbot's play was re-enacted on the shores of the Annapolis Basin near the site of the original performance.

This play and feast were undoubtedly the impetus that led to the founding by Champlain of the Order of Good Cheer. This Order that lasted only during the ensuing winter is referred to hereafter.

The land grant referred to in the prior Chapter that de Monts had given to Poutrincourt provided fishing and fur-trading rights. Henry IV ratified the grant in 1606. Poutrincourt was appointed Lieutenant Governor of Acadia and in charge of Port Royal to which he returned that same year.

In 1606 Poutrincourt, accompanied by Hébert and Champlain, explored the New England coastline as far south as Cape Cod with a view to establishing a colony there in place of the Port Royal site. In the short time that they were in the New England area, a clearing was seeded with Hébert's assistance in order to assess the productivity of the land. However because of unfriendly natives the idea of a settlement there was scotched and nothing came of this experiment.

At Port Royal Poutrincourt had a mill constructed to grind grain, and also had other buildings erected by the carpenters, joiners, masons and other tradesmen who had come from France with him. A water mill, a furnace and two small boats were also built.

One of Poutrincourt's first directions given after his return to Port Royal was to have crops sown and vegetables planted. These included wheat, rye, corn, flax, radishes, cabbage, and other produce.

Lescarbot himself tilled the ground and sowed "corn and kitchen herbs". Lescarbot noted that Poutrincourt looked to Louis Hébert to assist with the sowing and planting. He added that

.... our apothecary Master Louis Hébert [was] a man who, besides his experience in his art, takes great pleasure in tilling the land.

Lescarbot mentions Hébert a number of other times in his work. He repeated elsewhere that "our apothecary, Master Louis Hébert, [was] most sufficient in his art". In another chapter he stated that Hébert was "desirous to inhabit in these countries", a prescient foretelling of Hébert's destiny in New France.

In Volume I (1492-1849) of his book *Building the Canadian Nation*, the University of Toronto history professor George W. Brown wrote:

The early years of Port Royal are full of interest.... here came Louis Hébert, an apothecary from Paris, who was later to be the first farmer at Quebec. Canadian agriculture and medicine may perhaps, without too much exaggeration, be said to have begun with him.

During his time in Port Royal, Hébert searched for medicinal plants. In his book Abbé Després mentioned that Hébert had knowledge of botany that enabled him to gather plants from the interior lands, the hills, and the riverbanks. He studied these specimens to find ways of putting them to scientific use.

As a botanist his efforts in this regard contributed to the advancement of this science. Botany was then in its early stages. He also consulted with the natives to learn about the plants and herbs they used in their folk medicine.

The book *Great Moments in Pharmacy*, stated that Hébert examined drug plants brought to him at Port Royal by friendly Micmacs. The Micmacs were and are aboriginal peoples living in the Maritime Provinces and the Gaspé Peninsula.

The folk medicine plants they took to him and whose medicinal properties they taught him included boneset (eupatorium perfoliatum), mullein (verbascum thapsus), jack-in-the- pulpit (arisaema triphyllum), and golden seal (hydrastis canadensis).

Boneset was one of the foremost plants used by the natives. It was used as an antidote to the poison of the umbelliferous plant (now commonly known as water hemlock); it was also used as a remedy for typhoid fever. Mullein is an herbaceous plant with wooly leaves and yellow flowers. The flowers were boiled in water to make a tea which was taken for lung complaints.

Jack-in-the-pulpit is a small woodland plant whose roots were boiled in water to make a tea that the natives drank to allay stomach aches. Golden seal is a buttercup plant with a thick yellow rootstock which was utilized for bleeding and skin problems. The natives also used it as a yellow dye and pesticide.

Hébert, unlike many Europeans, did not perceive the Indians as dullards; rather he knew that while they lacked the sophistication of a Parisian upbringing they were a bright, intelligent race. He emphasized this point in his last words on his deathbed. He may have known how native folk medicine had saved the lives of many of Jacques Cartier's crew in 1535 when they were suffering from scurvy. If this was so, his admiration for the natives would have been further enhanced.

The *Canadian Geographic* issue of March/April 1999 also states that:

.... the first recorded hemp crop in North America was planted in 1606 near the Nova Scotia shore of the Bay of Fundy by French botanist and apothecary Louis Hébert.

During one of Poutrincourt's exploration trips with Hébert, the natives brought to him juicy grapes as well as fish to exchange for goods. Because of their quality and potential as a crop, Hébert uprooted a number of the wild vines on which these luscious grapes grew, intending to plant them in Port Royal. However due to an oversight on their departure the vines were left behind much to the chagrin of all, including Poutrincourt.

Lescarbot relates an incident that demonstrates the bravery of Hébert as well as others. One morning about dawn during an excursion, unfriendly natives attacked the French sentinels and killed two of them.

The other sentinels cried out and a number of Poutrincourt's men hastily arose without properly dressing and rushed to their shallop in order to save their night guards. The natives quickly fled. Among the men who came to the rescue of the sentinels were Hébert and Champlain as well as Robert Pontgravé (son of François), and Pierre Angibaut *dit* Champdoré (the marine pilot).

Subsequently Champlain attempted to kidnap some natives in Stage Harbor, Cape Cod. His purpose was not only to avenge the killing of the sentinels, but also to put them to work as slaves to operate the unpopular manually operated mill at Port Royal. However, the crafty natives foiled Champlain's plot.

Life at Port Royal must have been fairly pleasant for the men from France. Lescarbot states that the workmen had some free time each day and they would harvest lobsters, crabs, cockles, mussels and wild fowl. He added that everyone had "three quarts of pure and good wine a day". Perhaps this ample allotment made them wine lovers like many Frenchmen today.

The food ration meted out to the inhabitants of Port Royal included fish, beans, peas, rice, raisins, and prunes. There were further excursions by boat to check out other areas, to meet with the natives, to exchange goods for furs, and to explore.

The highlight in the winter of 1606-07 for a select few of the inhabitants of Port Royal (15 men since the role of each as steward reoccurred every 15 days) was L'Ordre de bons temps - the Order of Good Cheer. Following *Le Théâtre de Neptune* staged on November 16, 1606 at Port Royal by Lescarbot with its sumptuous banquet, Champlain established the Order of Good Cheer.

This Order was the first recorded social club and fraternity in North America. It is described both by Lescarbot and by Champlain. The purpose of the Order was to provide a festive occasion each evening for its members.   Each member of the Order was in turn commissioned to go hunting, to bring back the finest game and fish, and to have the cook prepare a lavish feast so that all might make merry.

According to Champlain, each designated chief steward for a particular evening "vied with each other to see who could do the best".   So much food was acquired and prepared that there was enough left over for breakfast and lunch the next day.

At each banquet feast the Chief Steward for the evening paraded in with a napkin on his shoulder, the wand of office in his hand, and the collar of the Order (which had ceremoniously been presented to him the previous night) dangling from his neck.   Marching gaily behind him in single file into the banquet room (in Poutrincourt's home) were the members of the Order, many bearing a savory dish on huge platters held shoulder high.

This jolly procedure, but with less of a flourish, was performed again with the dessert.   A fitting motto for the Order would have been "Eat, drink, and be merry" for the food was plentiful, the wine flowed freely, and the air was filled with jubilant songs.   At the end of the festivities the Chief Steward turned over to the next evening's steward the collar of the Order, each drank a cup of wine to the other, all present gave thanks to God, and the night of revelry and camaraderie was at an end.

Charles W. Jefferys, A.R.C.A., was an esteemed Canadian artist, who drew many creative illustrations portraying the human side of historical events in the early days of Canada.   There is a picture of the Order of Good Cheer done many decades ago by Jefferys depicting a parade into the banquet hall by the smiling members of the Order of Good Cheer.

There are two musicians, one playing a viola and the other a clarinet.   Seated on one side of the room watching the celebration is an elderly Indian smoking a long pipe. He apparently is a representation by Jefferys of Membertou, the Grand Chief of the Micmac who was a great warrior and a renowned shaman. Lescarbot said Membertou was a prophet among his people and one who could see well although he was over 100 years old, and who had even met Jacques Cartier. Lescarbot added:

> .... we had always twenty or thirty savages, men, women, girls and boys, who beheld us doing our offices. Bread was given them gratis, as we do here to the poor. But as for the Sagamos Membertou and other Sagamos (when any came to us) they sat at table eating and drinking as we did; and we took pleasure in seeing them
> ....

Charles W. Jefferys also did a creative representation of Lescarbot's play "Le Théâtre de Neptune" that Jefferys titled "The First Play in Canada, 1606".

Louis Hébert was enraptured with the beauty of Acadia. The hills, forests, rivers, meadows, and streams enchanted him and he found there a sense of freedom and a love of the land. No doubt the gaiety of the Order of Good Cheer contributed to his well-being during the long cold months of the winter in which these banquets were held.

However some French merchants, fur-traders and hatters were jealous of de Monts' trading monopoly. Over the winter months they influenced the anti-colonial Duc de Sully, Chief Minister of Henry IV, to have the King revoke the Patent of de Monts in 1607. As a result the heartbroken Poutrincourt, Hébert, Champlain, and the other men abandoned Port Royal and they returned to France in the autumn of 1607.

Almost simultaneously in that year, a group of colonists from England were sailing into Virginia to establish a colony not far from the abandoned Roanoke Colony. This was the site where Sir Walter Raleigh was unsuccessful in establishing a permanent settlement in the 1580s.

Shortly after the French colonists from Port Royal had returned to France, Poutrincourt had an audience with the King. He displayed to the King corn, wheat, oats, and other fruits and vegetables from the rich Acadian soil.

This produce had been grown and harvested with Hébert's assistance. Poutrincourt also presented the King with five "bustards" (long-legged game birds that were likely Canada geese or wild turkey) that he had brought back from Acadia. The King was pleased with these gifts and sent the game birds to Fontainebleau, a regal palace near Paris.

The King must have been impressed because in due course he decided to proceed with further efforts at settlement. Accordingly the trading privileges of de Monts were reinstated under another royal charter. As noted in the next Chapter de Monts concentrated his exploration and fur trading in the vicinity of the St. Lawrence River and the area that is now known as Quebec. De Monts placed Champlain in charge of this venture.

However it was Poutrincourt (who had been enamored by Port Royal and had received the land grant of Acadia from de Monts) who organized the next expedition to Acadia. For various reasons, Poutrincourt's return to Port Royal was delayed until 1610. His two sons, Charles and Jacques, also went to Port Royal.

Louis Hébert, who had been practicing as an apothecary in Paris since returning to France in 1607, also returned to Port Royal in 1610. A number of historians, such as Morris Bishop and Abbé Després, write that Hébert's wife Marie Rollet and Poutrincourt's wife also came to Port Royal, adding that these were the first two French women to walk on the soil of New France. They apparently arrived in 1611, as did two Jesuit priests, Fathers Biard and Massé.

The winter of 1610-11 was harsh and food was scarce. The melting of the snow and the end of winter were warmly welcomed. Spring saw the clearing of land, sowing of crops and planting of gardens. Everyone's spirits picked up considerably. Poutrincourt placed his son Charles de Biencourt in charge of Port Royal when he returned to France in 1611 in an endeavour to raise funds for the colony.

Louis Hébert's third stay in Acadia was from 1610 to 1613. While in the colony Louis Hébert not only planted a garden and sowed crops, he acted as the apothecary and as a physician.

He also performed other duties as needed. For example, in 1611 Hébert was instructed by Poutrincourt's son (who was in charge at Port Royal in his father's absence) to capture Robert Pontgravé (son of François).

Although the year before Robert had kidnapped a native girl and had later been excused for his conduct, it was subsequently discovered that he was scheming to overthrow Poutrincourt. Hébert with a group of men proceeded to Robert's post on the St. John River, but he was not there when the Hébert party arrived to arrest him. Subsequently, Robert was pardoned after swearing loyalty to Poutrincourt.

The nearby natives respected Hébert for his medical knowledge. Not only did he confer with them on their traditional healing practices, he also cultivated the natural herbs and medicines that they had introduced him to.

When the elderly Membertou was quite ill, he consulted Hébert for medical attention. Hébert did what he could for him, even cooking meals, but Membertou died. Prior to his death Membertou, his wife, children and grandchildren became Christians.

The account of Membertou's death in the *Jesuit Relations* of 1616 states:

> He died a very good Christian, and his death greatly saddened the Jesuits, for they loved him, and were loved by him in return. ... The Savages have no recollection of ever having had a greater or more powerful Sagamore.... would to God that all the French were as circumspect and prudent as he was.

In 1985, a monument honoring Membertou was erected at the Port Royal National Historic Site, which was created by the Canadian Government in 1940.

In France, a new company was formed in 1612 to establish another colony in Acadia some distance from Port Royal. Ladies at the French royal court were the impetus behind this new endeavour and provided financial support. Madame Antoinette de Guercheville, of whom the King had once been enamored, was the principal leader of this group. Madame de Guercheville had become fervent in her desire to have the natives converted to Catholicism. She had also become an ardent supporter and patron of the Jesuits in their missions.

St. Ignatius Loyola and others had founded the Jesuits in 1534. The Counter-Reformation, a reform movement, had arisen in the Roman Catholic Church in the 16th century as a response to the Protestant Reformation. The Jesuits had been in the vanguard of this movement.

In 1612, Madame de Guercheville had declined Champlain's plea for financial assistance to have Jesuits come to Quebec. She did so because Champlain's superior Sieur de Monts was a Huguenot. However, she contributed 1,000 ecus to the new venture in Acadia in which she was involved.

For this investment she was to share in the profits and the lands other than from Poutrincourt's Port Royal. She also ensured that the Jesuits would be intimately involved in this project. The expedition set out in March 1613 under the command of Réne le Coq de la Saussaye. On board were two Jesuits, Father Quentin and Brother Gilbert du Thet. On arriving at Acadia, de la Saussaye met with Hébert who was in charge of Port Royal in the absence of Charles de Biencourt.

De la Saussaye delivered letters from the Queen that directed the Jesuits who were already there (Fathers Pierre Biard and Ennemond Massé) to accompany de la Saussaye to the new colony. The following is an account of the arrival of de la Saussaye and his party by Father Biard in the Jesuit Relations:

> At Port Royal they found only five persons, that is the two Jesuits, their servant, the apothecary Hébert, and one other. Sieur de Biencourt and his other men were a long

way off some here, some there. Because Hébert was taking the Sieur's place, they presented him with the letters from the Queen which ordered that the Jesuits be released and permitted to go where they wished. So the Jesuits removed their possessions peacefully. And on that day and the day following they made it as agreeable for Hébert and his 'compagnon' [i.e. companion or mate - presumably his wife Marie Rollet who had come to Acadia a few years earlier] as they could, in order that their coming would not cause sadness. On departing (although they didn't need anything) they left a barrel of bread and some flagons of wine, so that their goodbye might likewise be made gracefully.

The Jesuit Relations were narratives written in French by the Jesuit missionary priests relating accounts of many happenings in New France and in Acadia in the 17th century. These Relations, that provide narrative accounts of daily life and occurrences, are a documentary wellspring of early Canadian history.

They were printed in Paris and eagerly read by many of the educated class throughout France. The documentation was prodigious. The later 19th century English translation under the editorship of R. G. Thwaites comprises dozens of volumes.

The new settlement established by de la Saussaye in 1613 did not last long. It had been set up near the Penobscot River on the Ile des Monts Déserts, an area that was a subject of dispute between France and England. That summer Samuel Argall, an Englishman from Virginia, attacked and conquered this settlement.

Depending on the source Argall has been called an adventurer, a freebooter, an admiral, a buccaneer, and a deputy-governor of Virginia. Perhaps he was all five at once. Earlier in that year of 1613 while Argall was sailing up the Potomac River near Virginia he kidnapped Pocahontas (a Powhatan Indian princess) and took her to Jamestown. There she later married a colonist, John Rolfe.

Argall took many of de la Saussaye's settlers to Virginia, promising to let them return to France sometime in the future. However when the English governor in Jamestown found out that there was a French colony at Port Royal, he ordered Argall to return to Acadia and raze that settlement.

Unprepared for a sneak attack, Port Royal was easy prey and Argall's men put the torch to it that very year. However before doing so he stripped the fort down to "the boards, bolts, locks and nails" and took horses as well. So wrote an onlooker Father Pierre Biard, the Jesuit priest who had arrived in Acadia in 1611.

The colonists and Louis Hébert in particular were devastated. Hébert's hard but satisfying work of clearing the land, tilling the earth, sowing crops and planting gardens was for naught. His dreams of planting himself permanently on the Canadian soil were dashed.

Hébert and his wife Marie Rollet returned to Paris that year with heavy hearts. Hébert realized that he would be going back to the more constricted life of a Parisian apothecary. He would no longer have his own fields and gardens to plant and the abundant harvests they would have produced; nor would he have the sense of freedom and liberty that he felt in the New World. As Julia Jarvis wrote in her monograph titled *Louis Hébert:*

> Madame Hébert loved the country no less than her husband... They lived happily and comfortably in Port Royal until the year 1613, when an English buccaneer sailed up from Virginia and captured and burnt the settlement.

Poutrincourt was in France when his Acadian colony was destroyed. His life came to an end several years later during the civil hostilities in France.

The English were now in control of Acadia. Some years later a Scot, Sir William Alexander, established a Scottish settlement. While commenting that there was a New England, a New France and a New Amsterdam, Alexander named the area Nova Scotia ("New Scotland"). However in 1632 the Treaty of Saint-Germain-en-Laye saw England return Acadia to France and Alexander's Scottish settlement came to an end. Consequently the French colony of Acadia was re-established. In the last half of the 17th century and into the 18th century it changed hands between the French and the English on several occasions.

In 1713 Acadia finally became a colony of Great Britain pursuant to the Treaty of Utrecht that ended the War of the Spanish Succession. Under this Treaty France retained Prince Edward Island (Île St. Jean) and Cape Breton, while Britain obtained the Hudson Bay trading area, Newfoundland and much of Acadia including Port Royal. However, relatively few people from Britain or New England relocated to Acadia subsequent to this Treaty, and the settlers there continued to be predominantly French Acadians.

By the 1750s there were over 10,000 French Acadians living in this area. These people generally refused to swear an oath of allegiance to the British crown, resulting in serious irritation to the ruling authorities. This led to a decision by the British authorities to carry out a mass deportation in 1755 of most of the Acadian population, as a final solution to this problem of the Acadians lack of allegiance to the English Crown.

Under this expulsion, many of the French Acadians were shipped or marched south into the United States as far as Virginia. Many were transported back to France and others were sent to the Caribbean. A few found their way back to Canada.

Many others traveled further south and settled in Louisiana in the Mississippi Basin. Robert Cavelier de La Salle had explored and claimed this Louisiana area for France in 1682. At a later date, in 1803, France sold this region to the United States pursuant to the Louisiana Purchase.

Acadian influence continues to this day in Louisiana. The word "Cajun", a corruption of Acadian, today has several meanings. The term is applied to the descendants of the French Acadians living in the Louisiana area. It also means their local dialect or patois, and it is also applied to their unique brand of cuisine.

Subsequent to the British expulsion of the French from Acadia in 1755, the Seven Years War of 1756 to 1763 occurred between several European countries. This led to the British Conquest of 1763 in which the French holdings in Canada came under the permanent control of England.

The next Chapter deals with early Quebec and de Monts' instructions to Champlain to establish a fur trading post there in 1608. This led Champlain to invite Louis Hébert and his family to come to Quebec.

Chapter Reference Sources

* "Biencourt de Poutrincourt et de Saint Just, Jean de" in the *Dictionary of Canadian Biography,* in collaboration with Hula Ryder, Vol. 1, *p. 96-97.*
* *Building the Canadian Nation - 1492-1849* by George W. Brown, Vol. I, p. 68.
* *Canada - The Foundation of its Future* by Stephen Leacock, p. 51-52.
* *Canadian Encyclopedia, The* editor in chief James H. Marsh, p. 11-12; 233.
* *Champlain's Order of Good Cheer* by L. M. Fortier, p. 9-12; 23-28.
* *Champlain: The Life of Fortitude* by Morris Bishop, p. 46: 92-93; 233.
* "Field of Opportunity" by Phil Jenkins in the *Canadian Geographic* magazine issue of March/April 1999, p. 61.
* *Great Moments in Pharmacy* by George A. Bender, p. 73.
* *History of Medicine in the Province of Quebec* by Maude Abbott, p. 15.
* *Jesuit Relations* by Father Pierre Biard, Vol. III, p. 205; 231-35; 261-63; Vol. IV p. 45-53.
* *Louis Hébert* by Julia Jarvis, p. 9-14.
* *Louis Hébert - Premier Colon Canadien et sa Famille* by Abbé Azarie Couillard Després, p. 23-35.
* *Nova Francia - A Description of Acadia, 1606* by Marc Lescarbot (extracted from his *Histoire de la Nouvelle France*), p.13; 35; 42-43; 61; 72; 74; 93; 95-96; 104; 107; 109; 117-19; 122; 125; 129; 133: 142; 271-72; 292.
* *Pioneers of France in the New World* by Francis Parkman, Vol. Two p. 107-08; 128 *et seq.*
* "Partners in Trade" segment of *Origins, A History of Canada* television documentary.

- *Samuel de Champlain - Father of New France* by Samuel Eliot Morison, p. 83; 89; 92; 94-97; 271.
- *White and the Gold - the French Regime in Canada, The* by Thomas B. Costain, p. 60-61; 112-13.

Chapter VIII

EARLY NEW FRANCE

In the 17th and 18th centuries, the broad meaning of the term "New France" embraced all of the French possessions in North America. These included Acadia and the St. Lawrence Valley in Canada as well as Louisiana and the Mississippi Valley in the United States. However, the discussion in this Chapter focuses on the St. Lawrence River area of New France in the 17th century and on the activities there in the earlier parts of that century.

The explorations of John Cabot, Giovanni da Verrazano and Jacques Cartier on behalf of France have previously been mentioned. The activities of Pierre du Gua de Monts and Jean de Biencourt de Poutrincourt have also been discussed.

After de Monts ceded his rights in Acadia to Poutrincourt he turned his attention to the St. Lawrence River area. This river flows some 1,200 kilometers northeast from Lake Ontario into the Gulf of St. Lawrence. Cartier, of course, had explored eastern parts of that area decades before.

After returning from a journey west to Hochelaga situated at the site of where the St Lawrence and Ottawa Rivers meet (now Montreal), Cartier spent the winter of 1535-36 near Stadacona (an Iroquois village, now the site of Quebec City).

In 1608 de Monts' fur-trade monopoly was renewed for one year on the basis that he would establish a colony in Canada. He engaged the services of Champlain and directed him to set up a fur-trading post at Quebec. Champlain had earlier worked for de Monts as a cartographer at Port Royal without any significant authority in that position.

Champlain set sail for the St. Lawrence area with a crew of fur traders, clerks, carpenters, and tradesmen. No women and no settlers accompanied him. The establishment of a fur-trading fort by Champlain in 1608 under de Monts' authorization was the commencement of the administration of New France by merchant companies for more than half a century. These companies proved to be more interested in the fur trade than in colonization.

Champlain was born in Brouage, France in 1567 where his father was a fisherman. He was probably christened as a Protestant since Protestants customarily conferred Old Testament names on their children, whereas a Catholic child was usually named after a saint. As well his birthplace, Brouage, was then a Huguenot city. However he was a Catholic at the time of his voyages to Acadia and New France.

He served in the French Wars of Religion between the Catholics and the French Huguenots under Henry IV. The King brought the conflicts to an end in 1598 by issuing the Edict of Nantes which granted toleration to Protestants.

Champlain's first trip to New France was in 1603 as a geographer and map maker. This was an expedition up the St. Lawrence River led by François du Pontgravé on behalf of a royal monopoly held by Aymar de Chaste and other French merchants. Champlain's subsequent sojourn in Acadia, his organization of the Order of Good Cheer, and his explorations in the area have been referred to in another Chapter.

In 1608 he and his party arrived at the site of what is now the modern-day city of Quebec ("the place where the river narrows" in the Algonquin language). This site was situated on the north shore of the St. Lawrence River at its juncture with the St. Charles River.

There Champlain had his workers construct the fort that was called L'Habitation. It was built in a locale that was eventually to become the first permanent settlement by Europeans in Canada. This was so notwithstanding the obstinate antagonism of his fur-trading masters and their successors - who viewed the term "fur-trade settlement" as an oxymoron.

The Habitation was constructed near the edge of the St. Lawrence River. It was three stories high with living quarters for the employees, separate accommodations for

Champlain, a storehouse (primarily for furs), an armory, a kitchen, platforms for cannons, and other amenities. A gallery circled the living quarters, while a promenade fronted on a moat fifteen feet wide and six feet deep that surrounded the Habitation and for which a drawbridge had been constructed.

In the years following his arrival, Champlain laid the foundation for a French fur empire in this emerging era of capitalism and royal colonialism. Under the guidance of the natives, he and the Company employees checked out trade routes and set up a huge native network to acquire furs. In addition they gave military support to the Hurons and the Algonquins in their tribal wars against the Iroquois.

Together the Hurons and the Algonquins formed a large group of aboriginal peoples, many of whom lived at that time in the areas of Quebec and Ontario where furs were plentiful. The Iroquois were a league or an alliance of First Nations tribes that included the Mohawk, Seneca, Onondaga, Cayuga and Oneida peoples. They were fierce warriors and shared a common language, Iroquoian, which the Hurons also spoke. Decades earlier the Iroquois had been driven out of Stadacona, Hochelaga and nearby areas by the Algonquins and were now living south and southeast of Lake Ontario.

Champlain's efforts at this time were primarily directed to the fur trade and to meeting the aims of those whom he served, the mercantile fur-trading companies in France. The objectives of these companies were profits from furs, not the establishment of a settlement. The obligation to colonize was an integral part of their royal monopoly grants as was their obligation to attempt to convert the aboriginals to Christianity. Nevertheless they played little heed to their duty to colonize.

When circumstances warranted, Champlain as the on-site person in charge at Quebec could show an iron fist in managing the Fort. Not long after his arrival in 1608, he learned of an insurrection plotted by some of the malcontent Company employees. They planned to kill him and to turn the Fort over to the Spaniards or the Basques for money. However one of the conspirators, Antoine Natel, informed Champlain of the plot. Champlain dealt severely with the lead instigator, a locksmith named Jean Duval. In a merciless display of frontier justice, Champlain had Duval decapitated. He then had Duval's head thrust on a pike and placed at the highest point of the Fort for public display. The other schemers were promptly dispatched in irons to France. Champlain never faced this kind of problem again.

In 1609 the Hurons and the Algonquins wanted to be the exclusive native traders of furs with the Europeans in the St. Lawrence Valley and the Great Lakes areas. However their traditional enemies, the Iroquois, frequently attacked them and they called upon Champlain and his personnel to join them in a sneak foray into Iroquois territory.

Notwithstanding that the winter had been brutal and many of his men had died of scurvy and dysentery, Champlain determined to participate with them in this attack. He did so in order to forge an alliance with them. He believed this would maintain and advance the fur-trading ambitions of the European interests to whom he was obligated. Champlain and his men accompanied a band of Hurons, Algonquins and Montagnais into what is now the State of New York. On this expedition he first laid eyes on the lovely lake in Vermont that now bears his name.

Champlain brought with him his trusty arquebus, an early type of portable matchlock musket in which the powder charge was ignited by a match or slow burning fuse. On encountering the Iroquois, Champlain shot and killed several of them. He later drew a sketch of the scene in which he is aiming and firing his arquebus at the Iroquois. The Iroquois had never experienced these "sticks of thunder" and when they witnessed their awesome power they fled into the forest.

While the Iroquois were vanquished in this instance, the long-term result was to make them enemies not only of the Hurons and the Algonquins but of the French as well. The Iroquois formed an alliance with the Dutch fur traders in New York and obtained arms from them. This made them even more militant against their enemies. In turn Champlain persuaded the Hurons and the Algonquins to carry on their fur trading with the French. He did so by pledging to provide arms and assistance to them in their combats with the Iroquois.

These developments, as well as the desire of the European countries for furs, converted tribal warfare with bows and arrows into brutal battles of extermination using European firearms. It proved devastating to the natives. So did alcohol and the cataclysmic diseases which the Europeans brought to the Americas. The natives had no innate immunity for such maladies as smallpox, typhus, and measles.

During the winter of 1615-16, Champlain lived with the Hurons, not by choice but by necessity. To maintain the allegiance of the Hurons (who were essential for the fur trade) he acceded to their entreaties that he and other Frenchmen accompany them on another raid against the Iroquois. Champlain was wounded on this unsuccessful 1615 raid. He asked the natives to take him to Hochelaga, but they refused and he reluctantly had to spend the winter of 1615-16 with them in Huron Country.

This prevented him from returning to France for the fall and winter, seasons which he had spent in France every year for each of the previous six years and again did consecutively for a number of years thereafter. In fact, during his time in Quebec from 1608 until he died in 1635, Champlain actually spent more than half of the autumns and winters (and sometimes entire years) in France, not Quebec. Perhaps this seasonal lifestyle qualifies Champlain for the title of Canada's first snowbird.

Pontgravé was usually left in command when Champlain went exploring or during those times when he wintered or remained in France. Early on in New France and until the 1630s Champlain was still hoping to find the fabled route to the Orient.

Alienation of the Iroquois and alliance with the Hurons meant that henceforth the French would be drawn into their inter-tribal wars over many years. These wars often had disastrous consequences to the French.

The Iroquois frequently attacked the inhabitants of New France and their aboriginal allies. Many Frenchmen and Indians were massacred over subsequent years. In 1660 the heroic Adam Dollard des Ormeaux, commander of the fort at Ville-Marie (previously Hochelaga and now Montreal), was killed as were some of the settlers, Hurons and Algonquins.

Prior to that in 1649, the Iroquois had invaded leading Huron villages, routed the Hurons and forced them to disband. The Jesuit priest Jean de Brebeuf and other clergy were tortured and killed by the Iroquois when they were in Huron Country in 1649, the year that the Hurons were dispersed by the Iroquois.

There is an interesting long term consequence of the Iroquois antagonism to the French arising from Champlain's alliance with the Hurons. It was the killing of the only grandson of Louis Hébert by the Iroquois. This led indirectly to the extinguishment of direct descendants of Louis Hébert bearing his surname.

Two intriguing incidents of historic interest occurred in 1613. In the one of lesser significance, Champlain's astrolabe went missing on one of his travels. The word astrolabe is derived from Greek words meaning "star-taking" and was an instrument used to find the altitude of a star and to assist in navigation. It has since been replaced by the sextant.

An astrolabe was found near Cobden, Ontario in 1867 and is now held by the Canadian Museum of Civilization in Hull, Quebec. Some people believe that this is Champlain's missing astrolabe. However there is disagreement on its provenance and an article by Douglas Hunter in *The Beaver* magazine of December 2004/January 2005 states:

The Champlain provenance case for the "Cobden astrolabe" ..... appears so weak as to be ephemeral.

The other noteworthy event that happened in the year 1613 was the arrival from France of Guillaume Couillard. He came as a tradesman and a shipwright to work for the fur trading company.   An ensuing Chapter of this book describes his marriage to the daughter of Louis Hébert and Marie Rollet and the notable contributions that he and his wife made in Quebec.

Champlain was unmarried when he came to Quebec. However in 1610 he returned to France to marry Hélène Boullé, the daughter of a wealthy Huguenot, Nicholas Boullé. The daughter was given a dowry of 6,000 livres by her father. Hélène was a child-bride - only 12 years old, Champlain was then 43 years of age.   She became a Catholic.

Hélène apparently was most unhappy with what was surely an arranged marriage.   Over three years after the nuptials, fifteen year-old Hélène was still in Paris.

At that time she caused so much distress that her parents disinherited her and made public that she had vanished. Neither Champlain who was wintering in Paris nor her parents knew where she was. In due course she reappeared.

However it was not until the year of Champlain's death in 1635 that, as a Champlain biographer S. E. Morison writes, her parents "restored their errant daughter's rights of inheritance". Not long after Champlain's death, Hélène entered a convent run by Ursuline nuns where she died in 1654.

It is interesting to note that the marriage contract referred to Samuel **de** Champlain.   Up to this time Champlain's name did not include the "de", a term that indicates an honorable rank. His book *Des Savages* in 1603 did not show the "de".

It appears he merely assumed this title in later years. Perhaps, as one of his biographers Morris Bishop suggests, he did so "for the gratification of Hélène and his new family".   Hélène's family was a well-to-do bourgeois family, while Champlain's father had been a fisherman.

Champlain never received a noble title or honors from the two kings under whom he served or from Cardinal Richilieu. Samuel Morison also wrote that Champlain was not "strictly entitled" to be called either "Sieur" or use the title "de".   In his brief biography of Champlain in the *Dictionary of Canadian Biography,* Quebec historian Marcel Trudel writes that;

> .... one must accept with considerable caution the titles
> that Champlain assumed or allowed himself to be given.

In 1610, the same year as Champlain's marriage, a French explorer Etienne Brûlé, was sent by Champlain to live with the Hurons to learn their language. From time to time Champlain frequently sent young men to be with the Indians so that they could learn their language and act as interpreters.

Brûlé was likely the first coureur de bois and the first European to see three of the Great Lakes - Huron, Ontario and Superior. The term "coureur de bois" literally means "runner of the woods". It later came to mean a free-spirited French or Metis fur trader or trapper, often unlicensed, who roamed lands on the Canadian frontier where fur-bearing wildlife was plentiful.

Missionaries were sent to New France by the Catholic Church to proselytize among the aboriginals in the early part of the 1600s. In 1615 the Recollets arrived in Quebec in large part due to Champlain's efforts.   The Jesuits arrived in Quebec in 1625 but had been in Acadia prior to that date. They organized a mission in Huron Country, but the Hurons were reluctant targets and conversions in this period were slow.

At one point the Jesuits tried to induce native conversions by dissuading the French from providing the Indians with firearms unless they had become Christians. Lack of firearms made the Hurons more defenseless against Iroquois attacks.

The clergy knew efforts to convert future French settlers would be unnecessary since in 1628 Protestants were barred from settling in New France. In that year, Louis XIII's forces besieged La Rochelle, the port on the Atlantic coast of west France which was a Huguenot stronghold. The nine-year old Louis XIII had succeeded his father, Henry IV, as King of France in 1610.

From that time on only members of the Catholic faith could settle in New France. On the other hand Puritans, Protestants and French Huguenots settled in the colonies that were to become the United States.

While the fur-trade merchants wielded secular authority in New France, in the spiritual realm the Catholic Church was the exclusive power there. One of France's prime objectives in New France, in addition to defending its colonial holdings, was to convert the natives to Christianity.

Champlain left New France in 1629 since it had been conquered by the English. However Marie Rollet, the widow of Louis Hébert, and her family did not abandon their home and remained in Quebec. The English held possession until 1632 when it was reacquired by France.

After an absence of four years, Champlain sailed from France to Quebec in 1633. He was now designated the lieutenant for Cardinal Richelieu in New France. Richelieu, a French Roman Catholic dignitary and statesman, was the chief minister and influential policy adviser of Louis XIII.

Champlain, who was 66 years old when he returned to Quebec in 1633, was unaccompanied by his wife Hélène, who was now 35 years of age.

On Champlain's return a memorial chapel was built in Quebec in honor of the restoration of its colonies to France. Although it was named Notre Dame de la Recouverance, it was called the Champlain Chapel.

Champlain did not live long after he came back. He died on Christmas day 1635. He was interred in the

Champlain Chapel, but today the exact location of his burial site is problematic. More details as to Champlain's return to New France and his death are referred to in a later Chapter.

Champlain was a prolific writer. He wrote at length about his various travels. As a cartographer he drew maps of many places. *The Works of Samuel de Champlain* are most noteworthy.

However in his voluminous writings Champlain divulged little of significance relating to his personal life. For example, there is no reference to his marriage to Hélène.

No authentic portrait of Champlain exists. His exact features are unknown except as they appear in a rough sketch that he drew of himself firing his arquebus at the Iroquois in 1609. There is a portrait in existence which purports to be a likeness of Champlain, but it is a fraud painted by a French artist L. C. J. Ducornet.

In 1854 Ducornet reproduced the image, with some variations, of an engraving previously made by Balthasar Moncornet of a man named Michel Particelli. This engraving still survives.

Ducornet designated his deception "Champlain" and that fraudulent image is often represented as Champlain. For example, Abbé Després reproduced the fake picture in his book and identified it as Champlain, as did a number of other authors.

The fur trade, and to a lesser extent, fishing were the prime economic activities in New France during Champlain's time there. The French mercantile interests involved in these pursuits had no use for settlements and colonization in New France. They believed that settlers would not contribute in a significant way to the acquisition of furs and fish.

The merchants turned a blind eye to their legal duty to settle the land. They did not even pay lip service to their obligations in this respect. There is little doubt that they surreptitiously, or perhaps blatantly, discouraged the introduction of colonists. This attitude was exemplified in their dictatorial treatment of Louis Hébert discussed in the next Chapter.

Furs, particularly from the millions of beavers in the hinterland, were the economic engine of New France. The fur trade was to play a dominant role in the economy of Canada for well over two hundred years.

In August 1616 a Jesuit priest Father Charles Lalemant wrote in the *Jesuit Relations* of the different furs the natives brought to trade, and the goods the French gave them in exchange. The principal fur was that of the beaver but there were also hides of lynx, fox, otter, marten, etc. The merchandise the natives traded for the furs included cloaks, hatchets, iron arrowheads, swords, picks, knives, kettles, prunes, peas, and tobacco.

As furs in the Quebec area were depleted by over-trapping, the need for new sources became the economic spark for the westward exploration of Canada in the hunt for new habitats of fur-bearing animals. The immediate result of the French merchant company's concentration on fur profits and its antipathy to settlers was that nine years after Champlain had built the Habitation in Quebec there was not one farmer, not even one permanent settler in Quebec.

However, in 1617 this state of affairs was to change rather modestly number-wise but otherwise historically momentous. In Paris in 1616 Champlain encountered Louis Hébert, his old Acadian acquaintance and co-member of the Order of Good Cheer, and history was to be made. That meeting and its aftermath are the subject of ensuing Chapters.

Chapter Reference Sources

* *Beginnings of New France: 1524-1663, The* by Marcel Trudel, translation by Patricia Claxton, p. 75.
* *Canadian Encyclopedia, The* editor in chief James H. Marsh, p. 933; 1194; 1517; 1622.
* *Canadian Frontier, 1534-1760, The* by W. J. Eccles, p. 32-33.

- "Champlain, Samuel de" by Marcel Trudel in the *Dictionary of Canadian Biography*, Vol. I, p. 186-99.
- *Champlain: The Life of Fortitude* by Morris Bishop, p. 3; 112-13; 145 *et seq.*
- *Founding of Canada - Beginnings to 1815, The* by Stanley B. Ryerson, p. 82-85; 88-89.
- *In Search of Canada*, by Ronald C. Kirbyson, p. 69-72.
- *Jesuit Relations* by Father Charles Lalemant, Vol. IV, p. 207.
- *Louis Hébert - Premier Colon Canadien et sa Famille* by Abbé Azarie Couillard Després, p. 40.
- "Mystery of Champlain's Astrolabe, The" by Douglas Hunter in *The Beaver* Magazine Dec./04-Jan./05, p. 14-23.
- *Old Quebec - Trails and Homes* by E. C. Woodley, p. 14.
- "Partners in Trade" segment of *Origins, A History of Canada* television documentary.
- *Samuel de Champlain - Father of New France* by Samuel Eliot Morison, p. 17; 102 *et seq*; 130; 208; 216; 225.
- *Tercentenary History of Canada - From Champlain to Laurier, The* by Frank Basil Tracy, Vol. I, p. 52-53; 60; 62; 65-66.
- *White and the Gold - The French Regime in Canada, The* by Thomas B. Costain, p. 92-97.

Chapter IX

HÉBERT FAMILY TRAVELS TO NEW FRANCE

Perhaps Champlain's most notable achievement in advancing the future progress of New France was his invitation to Louis Hébert to come to the fort at Quebec City. They had first met when they were both members of the de Monts expedition to Acadia in 1604. In a 1914 article by M. Charlton in the *Johns Hopkins Hospital Bulletin* entitled "Louis Hébert", the author wrote:

> Louis Hébert, apothecary, surgeon, and agriculturist is regarded, next to Champlain, as the "Father of New France". When Champlain induced his old friend of Port Royal to venture once more to become a colonist of New France, he knew he had accomplished a greater work in building up his colony than had been done since its foundation. For Louis Hébert had proved his worth at Port Royal, not only as a surgeon, but as a keen and ardent agriculturist.

After the English burned Port Royal in 1613 and evicted the French, Hébert and his wife Marie Rollet had reestablished themselves in Paris on their return from Acadia. At the time of Champlain's approach to him in 1616, Hébert was practicing his profession as an apothecary in his Paris shop catering in large part to the pharmaceutical needs of the privileged French nobility. The fur-trading company was in need of an apothecary/physician for Quebec and Hébert obviously welcomed Champlain's overture. The thought of living in the New World, where he and his wife had previously spent happy years, must have filled him with hope and great expectations. The prospect of owning land, and the promise of a more fulfilling life, was an irresistible lure.

Champlain and Hébert knew each other well from their shared experiences in and around Acadia prior to Champlain leaving that area in 1607, and each held the other in high esteem. Champlain's principal motive in entreating Hébert to go to Quebec was was to obtain someone for the fort with the services and skills that Hébert could provide as its apothecary and physician. At that time it was not unusual for an apothecary to also frequently perform the duties of a physician.

Hébert saw Champlain's appeal to him as a God-given opportunity to return to the area he had lived in on three separate occasions between 1604 and 1613. He loved New France with a passion, and wished to settle there permanently. The allure of those virgin lands across the sea must have spoken loudly to his heart; the siren "call of the wild" must have been all but irresistible.

However, Hébert's romanticism was tempered by reality. He was now a middle-aged man, forty-two years old, with a wife and three children. He was determined to take his family with him to that magnificent country beyond the seas. He did not intend to live in New France separate and apart from his wife and children.

Unlike Champlain, whose wife resided in Paris at the time, Hébert would not live in Quebec while his wife and children were thousands of miles away in Paris. In addition he wanted his own plot of land to clear, to till, to sow crops, to plant gardens, and to grow herbs and vegetables.

At the time of his invitation to him, Champlain would have received this message from Hébert. To entice Louis to come to Quebec, Champlain offered impressive terms to Hébert on behalf of the Company of Canada, by whom Champlain was employed. The Company of Canada was established in France in 1613 (under the Prince de Condé, Viceroy of New France) to take over the fur-trading monopoly that de Monts' company previously held. It was formed by Condé and leading merchants of Rouen, LaRochelle and St. Malo. Under its Charter it undertook to convey a number of families to New France as colonists.

De Monts had no active position in the Company of Canada. His prior essential role in spearheading the founding of Quebec has not received the attention it deserves. It was he who equipped the ship *Le Don de Dieu* and financed the expedition to Quebec in 1608 to found a permanent trading center at that location. De Monts was the individual who spearheaded the venture and hired Champlain to go to Quebec for that purpose. Without de Monts' financial support and backing Quebec would not have been founded at this time; Champlain on his own could not have accomplished this historical achievement.

It was de Monts who had the vision and foresight to establish a fort in Quebec, at a site that he had first visited in the year 1600. De Monts, a Huguenot, deserves to be recognized as one of the prime Fathers of New France. In *The Beginning of New France*, Marcel Trudel wrote:

> Without de Monts, it can easily be imagined that there would have been no Champlain.

On behalf of the Company of Canada, Champlain offered Hébert a salary of 200 crowns per year (not an insubstantial sum in those days) for his services as an apothecary and physician for the Company. In addition, Hébert would be permitted to bring his wife and family to Quebec and they would be provided with maintenance for a period of three years. As well, Hébert would receive a land concession of 10 arpents for the use of himself and his family. An arpent was an old French unit of land measurement equal to about one acre.

Undoubtedly, Hébert would have discussed this proposal with his wife. He surely would have verbally painted a picture of the golden opportunity with which they had been presented. He decided to accept Champlain's offer because it promised the conditions upon which he wished to return to New France with his wife and family.

In preparation for the move to Quebec in 1617 Hébert wound up his Parisian practice as an apothecary, sold his shop, disposed of his property, and packed those family belongings that were to be taken overseas with them. His wife and three children and their servant Henri headed to Honfleur, the French port of embarkation. En route to the port they had high hopes and expectations about the new life they were shortly to begin on the far side of the Atlantic Ocean.

However, when they arrived at Honfleur they were confronted by an untoward and shocking surprise. The Boyer element was now in charge of the Company of Canada. The Company's interest was in fur profits, not settlers. Although Champlain was in France, he was not present in Honfleur and was not a party to the Company's confrontation with Hébert. The Company told Hébert in no uncertain terms that Champlain did not have the power or authority to agree to the salary of 200 crowns per year and other terms that Hébert had relied on in making this momentous decision to return to New France.

Hébert effectively was now homeless (as were his wife, children and servant). Having disposed of his business back in Paris, he was told what terms the Company was unilaterally imposing on him if he was to continue with his move to Quebec. Unknown to Hébert, Boyer had prepared a new written contract in advance and presented it to Hébert at Honfleur. Prior to Hébert and his family being permitted to sail to Quebec, Boyer required him to execute it as is.

The revised agreement arbitrarily provided for a reduced salary for Hébert. Instead of 200 crowns per annum, as Champlain had promised him, Hébert was to be paid only 100 crowns annually for three years. In addition, his land concession was reduced.

As well, the family and his servant Henri must serve the Company without any remuneration whatsoever. Another condition was that Hébert would be required to assist with all his power any one who was sick, without receiving any payment for doing so. Also Hébert would be prohibited from trading with the natives and taking part in the fur trade. A further requirement was that Hébert was to sell to the Company, at prices prevalent in France, any agricultural products or produce harvested by him which were in excess of his own families needs.

With his family and personal belongings, Hébert had arrived at Honfleur ready and willing to leave his Parisian relatives and friends and eager for an exhilarating new life thousands of kilometers away. It was then as he was ready to sail for his new homeland that the Company gave him this take-it-or-leave-it contract.

The manner in which the fur trade merchants flagrantly treated him and his family was shameful and unethical. It was a most inauspicious beginning to this pioneer family's journey to make a permanent home in Canada. The Company was rude, lewd and crude.

Hébert was no doubt deeply hurt and distressed at the gross and cavalier manner in which he and his family were treated by the Company. Having burned his bridges in Paris, he made a decision that the family would carry on with their plans and the life they had dreamed of. He signed the unfair contract on March 6, 1617.

Shortly after the contract was signed, the ship set sail for New France carrying the Hébert's to their new destiny. The ocean crossing was not comfortable and proved to be not only scary but dangerous. Ships in those days were radically different from the cruise ships of today. Crossing the Atlantic Ocean took weeks, not days, in a cramped wooden vessel that sometimes seemed like a prison.

These ships were much smaller and often leaked, resulting in the bilge collecting filthy, unhealthy water and frequently the air reeked from the stagnant fluid. Vermin on board was not unheard of.

Without modern washrooms and toilet facilities, sanitation and personal hygiene left much to be desired. Without refrigeration fresh food was quickly consumed after departure, leaving an unhealthy diet of dried or salted rations; fresh water ran out within a week after departure, leaving barely potable water for the remainder of the trip. There were no air conditioners, no motors to speed up the long dreary crossing, no modern gyrostabilizers to significantly level the side-to-side rolling of the ship.

The ocean crossing could also be daunting and hazardous due to storms, winds and towering waves. Icebergs cloaked in fog, and the perilous currents and rocks of the St. Lawrence Gulf and the St. Lawrence River, could be further dangers in the latter part of the voyage. As well, there was a constant fear of roving pirates with their marauding corsairs.

The precise conditions of the ship in which the Héberts journeyed to Quebec are not known, but would not have been too dissimilar to those outlined above. However some details of their long and stormy voyage are known. While in a fog not far from Newfoundland, a violent storm pushed their ship against a mountainous ice floe so hard that it would seem the ship would sink. There was such concern that the voyagers said their confessions to Father Joseph Le Caron to prepare their souls to meet God.

Marie Rollet, realizing the great peril they were in, lifted her young son Guillaume through the ship's hatch so that he could be blessed by Father LaCaron. It seemed miraculous that there was no shipwreck and that they all survived this harrowing experience. The Recollet brother Gabriel Sagard wrote that after 13 weeks of navigation the ship and its passengers arrived at Tadoussac "after having been in continual fear of death and fatigue they couldn't take any more."

Tadoussac was a village on the north shore of the St. Lawrence River at the mouth of the Saguenay River, about 200 kilometers northeast of the fort at Quebec. After arriving at Tadoussac, the exhausted newcomers remained there for a short time before proceeding on to their destination of Quebec.

Prior to leaving, on Sunday the Héberts went to Mass at Tadoussac with the sailors, tradesmen and other travelers. The small chapel was made of boughs of trees. It was decorated with wild flowers by Marie Rollet and the Hébert children, all of whom were devout Christians. This temporary stop at Tadoussac introduced the newcomers to another peril, countless stinging mosquitoes. The Recollet priest Father Paul Huet, who celebrated the Mass, had two of the ship's crew position themselves next to him waving branches to ward off the pesky critters. Sagard wrote that after dinner the group solemnly sang the vespers, and their Divine praises sounded to Heaven.

Some four centuries later, it is hard to envisage the difficult conditions faced by early inhabitants of New France. After an arduous and hazardous ocean crossing, the newcomers had to contend with harsh living conditions, extreme weather, warring natives and lack of the foods and comforts that they had enjoyed in Paris. It took a special kind of bold and courageous person to leave home, family and friends to venture far away to a sparse and undeveloped community in the backwoods of Canada, where there were negligible civilized amenities.

After a well-earned rest and with their energies recharged the Héberts left Tadoussac for Quebec, their final destination, and for the unknown future that lay before them.

Chapter Reference Sources

- *Backwoodswoman, The* by Isabel Skelton, chapter I, p. 12-13.
- *Beginnings of New France: 1524-1663, The* by Marcel Trudel, translation by Patricia Claxton, p. 67.
- *Champlain: The Life of Fortitude* by Morris Bishop, p. 232-33.
- *Early Trading Companies of New France, The* by H. P. Biggar, p. 105.
- *First Establishment of the Faith in New France* by Father Christian Le Clercq, translation by John G. Shea, p. 115-118.
- *Founder of New France: a Chronicle of Champlain, The* by Charles W. Colby, p. 76-77 .
- *Histoire du Canada* by Gabriel Sagard, p. 32-35.
- *In Search of Canada* by Ronald C. Kirbyson, p. 15.
- "Louis Hébert" by M. Charlton *"Johns Hopkins Hospital Bulletin"*, Vol. 25, 1914, p. 158.
- *Louis Hébert - Premier Colon Canadien et sa Famille* by Abbé Azarie Couillard Després, p. 42-44.
- *Samuel de Champlain - Father of New France* by Samuel Eliot Morison, p. 137; 147.
- *White and the Gold - the French Regime in Canada, The* by Thomas B. Costain, p. 90-91.

Chapter X

HÉBERT FAMILY SETTLES IN CANADA

Early in June 1617 Canada's pioneer Hébert family finally arrived at the fort that is now Quebec City. At that time Quebec was simply a small fur-trading outpost of the Company of Canada. The Company was owned and controlled by merchants and investors in France. The fur-trading post had a population of perhaps 50 people.

All of the men at the fort were employed by the Company of Canada and their activities were related directly or indirectly to the advancement of the fur trade business. They were prohibited from conducting personal business or establishing a farm.

Three of the men at the fort (Abraham Martin, Nicholas Pivert and Pierre Desportes) had brought their wives with them from France. Two of these had each brought a daughter, one of whom was Hélène Desportes who is mentioned hereafter. However, the author Morris Bishop noted that neither Champlain nor Sagard make mention of females in Quebec before 1616. This would indicate that it was 1617 before any women arrived in Quebec.

Nobody in this small and precarious population was a colonist or a farmer. The objectives of their employer, fur trade profits, precluded that status. This was so not withstanding that the absence of farms meant there were no crops of fresh vegetables and fruits for the employees of the trading post. The only local food was fish and game and wild berries; the rest of the food supply had to be imported from France.

The arrival of Louis Hébert and his family marked a new era, and signaled a new beginning, for Quebec. It now would have not only a man professionally gifted in helping sick people; it would have its first European family of permanent settlers and farmers. They were heroic trailblazers of paths to be subsequently emulated by millions of others.

Professor W. L. Morton in his book *The Kingdom of Canada* wrote concerning the early days of Quebec:

> Of true colonists there were few: chief among them was Louis Hébert, an apothecary turned farmer who had already tried the life of a colonist in Acadia.

The members of the Hébert family are the outstanding pioneers who laid the foundation for European and non-native settlement of the proud, free and magnificent nation that Canadians live in today.

On learning of the imminent arrival at Quebec of the ship transporting the Héberts, the people from the fort gathered near the shore to heartily greet these newcomers.

One can visualize the excitement with which the Héberts stepped on the soil of their new homeland, a land where they were determined and destined to spend the rest of their lives. A genteel, refined, and soft-hearted Hébert did not blame or hold a grudge against Champlain for the shabby and devious manner in which he had been treated by the officials of the fur-trading Company of Canada.

When these officials laid down the non-negotiable conditions to him at the port of Honfleur, Hébert would have realized that in this respect Champlain had little if any influence with his employers. Champlain, a servant of the Company, had no clout to make officials of the Company honor the agreement with Hébert that Champlain had struck on their behalf.

It would be interesting to know Champlain's inner reaction to the cads he worked for when he learned of their scandalous conduct in dealing with his old Acadian comrade Louis Hébert. Champlain knew, of course, that he had persuaded Hébert to come to Quebec on terms that had subsequently been dishonorably rejected by the men he took orders from.

In such circumstances it is not difficult to imagine that a subordinate, such as Champlain, might consider resigning from such an ignoble employer, particularly one who had placed no faith in his bargaining process with

Hébert. However, Champlain's own New World ambitions obviously outweighed that consideration in his mind.

After their arrival, the Héberts exchanged hearty greetings and pleasantries with the inhabitants of the fort. They then had to give some thought as to where they would sleep that night. Legend has it that the Héberts pitched a tent under an imposing elm tree at the corner of what is now Ste. Anne Road in Quebec City. This was to be their temporary abode for the next several months while they were building a permanent home.

Hébert wasted no time in choosing a site on his land concession on which to construct a home. In 1617 all buildings of the fort were built near the water's edge. In surveying his modest domain, with its wilderness background on the edge of the primeval forest, Hébert was innovative in deciding to build his home on the heights overlooking the river.

To do so he had to make a clearing on the crest of the cliff above the fort. He set about this with a purpose, not brooding over the skullduggery he and his family had endured prior to his departure from Honfleur.

Besides clearing the land for a home, Hébert wanted to find fertile soil and clear it for a garden and a farm. This was not an easy chore. The virgin forest in this untamed frontier contained gigantic walnut trees, mighty oaks, other huge trees and thick undergrowth.

Hébert's hewing tools for the task facing him were primitive by today's standards. Trees were chopped down, trunks were removed, the slash was burned and the land was cleared with a hatchet, a spade, a pick and a mattock.

A mattock was a tool similar to a pickaxe with a flat adze-shaped blade at each end of the head. It was used to loosen compact soil, to excavate and to cut roots, and for comparable activities. Hébert carried on with undaunted patience and persistence to prepare the concession for his farm.

Hébert cleared the land tree-by-tree, rock-by-rock, and foot-by-foot in order to cultivate crops, to grow vines, to plant an orchard and to have a garden. He tilled the soil and planted a variety of seeds, plants and an apple orchard (with trees brought from Normandy) in order to harvest from the land an assortment of fruits, vegetables and various herbs.

Hébert would conquer the land with an axe; not with a sword nor with a horse or plow, items that he did not possess. It was hard labor, often made more onerous by black flies and stinging mosquitoes, but it was a labor of love.

He was doing something by the sweat of his brow which would bring to life his dream of a home and a farm for himself and his family in the land he loved. He was assisted in this task by Henri, the servant whom he had brought with him from France, and occasionally by some of the employees from the fort. It is not hard to imagine that, to the extent of their abilities, his wife Marie Rollet and their children also pitched in.

Chapter Reference Sources

- *Canadian Frontier, 1534-1760, The* by W. J. Eccles, p. 24; 38.
- *Champlain: The Life of Fortitude* by Morris Bishop, p. 231.
- *Founder of New France: a Chronicle of Champlain, The* by Charles W. Colby, p. 67; 80-81.
- *Kingdom of Canada, The* by W. L. Morton, p. 32.
- *Louis Hébert - Premier Colon Canadien et sa Famille* by Abbé Azarie Couillard Després, p. 45-46; 50-51.
- *Old Quebec - Trails and Homes* by E. C. Woodley, p. 16-17.

Chapter XI

PIONEER LIFE OF THE HÉBERT FAMILY IN QUEBEC

When enough land had been cleared, Louis Hébert immediately set to work to construct a permanent home for himself and his family. Carpenters and masons from the fort helped him. In due course, the first pioneer home in Quebec of a permanent settler and his family stood proudly on the cliff above the fort.

It was a one-storey stone house measuring 38 feet by 19 feet. In it the Héberts placed the furniture and the belongings they had brought from their Parisian home. The devout Héberts invited the Recollet priest Father Joseph LeCaron (who had come from Honfleur on the same ship as them) to bless their home.

An English translation of an extract from a monograph titled *Louis Hebert, Premier colon du Canada* written by Laure Conan reads as follows:

> With what happiness did Hébert build and light the first fire in the hearth! How sweet was this hour. The flame of the hearth, the thousand small sounds which murmured from the blazing wood, filled the hearts of everyone with joy. Instead of a canvas tent soaked with dew, they finally had a solid roof over their heads in the comfort of heat and shelter.

On looking over the fruits of his labor, Hébert must have felt a quiet satisfaction. From the virgin forest in this frontier land he had carved out a clearing on which he had established a home, a garden, a vineyard and an orchard. Where once there had been a thick and untamed forest in the wild there was now shelter, growth, color, human enrichment and life flowing from this land.

The life-altering journey, hopes and dreams of Louis Hébert and Marie Rollet had come to fruition in Quebec. Only a few months before Hébert had been a mature, refined apothecary in his confined shop in the heart of Paris, a cultured city with hundreds of thousands of people.

There he had ground herbs with a mortar and pestle, concocting potions for the French aristocracy and nobility ensconced in their plush salons. Now he was a modest apothecary and neophyte pioneer farmer in the frontiers of Quebec with perhaps 50 unostentatious employees of a fur-trading post.

Now in the great outdoors of Canada Hébert tilled the land, sowed crops, and planted fruits, vegetables and herbs, as well as ministering to the medical needs of that tiny community in the harsh backwoods. At the same time Marie Rollet attended to the domestic needs of the family. She looked after the children, cooked the meals, washed the clothing, cleaned the house and helped with the agricultural chores of the homestead.

After one of his visits to the Hébert homestead Champlain, who had been accompanied by his dog Matelot, wrote:

> I inspected everything, the cultivated land which I found sown and filled with fine grain, the gardens full of all kinds of plants, such as cabbages, radishes, lettuce, purslane, sorrel, parsley and other plants, squash, cucumbers, melons, peas, beans and other vegetables as fine and as well forward as in France, together with the vines brought and planted here, already well advanced, in short everything increasing and growing visibly.

Subsequently Champlain wrote that on April 20, 1624, a violent gale caused damage to the gable of Hébert's stone house and that Champlain had arranged to have it rebuilt for him.

The Héberts socialized with a number of people from the fort and would invite them to their comfortable home on festive and other occasions. The three families whose husbands were employed by the fur-trading Company must have been frequent guests for dinners and good times.

These families were Pierre Desportes and his wife Marie Françoise Langlois and their daughter Hélène; Abraham Martin and his wife Marguerite Langlois and their daughter Anne; and Nicholas Pivert and his wife Marguerite Lesage and their niece. We know for certain of the close ties that developed with the Desportes family since their daughter Hélène later married Guillaume, the Hébert's only son.

Some years later in 1635 Abraham Martin acquired lands on the heights of Quebec. These lands became known as the Plains of Abraham. It was at this location on the 13th of September of 1759, that the Battle of the Plains of Abraham occurred between the English and the French. General James Wolfe led the English forces to victory over the French commanded by the Marquis de Montcalm.

When the Héberts arrived in Quebec, the young men at the fort would have noticed the attractive marriageable daughter Anne that came with them. As one of Champlain's biographers Morris Bishop wrote, Anne "caused a great refurbishing of shaving tackle".

In the winter time with the land covered by a mantle of snow and the rivers frozen over, the fur traders in the fort below munched on their smoked eels and salted pork. They must have contemplated with admiration (and perhaps a touch of envy) the industrious pioneer homesteaders on the cliff above them. The Hébert family would have been warmly and comfortably settled in their sturdy, cozy home, dining on a healthy variety of foods that they themselves had grown.

However, in lean winters when food was scarce the Héberts provided a good portion of their stored-up food supplies (which they themselves had harvested from their own crops) to the inhabitants of the fort. This proved a godsend in tough times.

Although Hébert's working heart was with his garden and farm, he was obliged to provide miscellaneous services to the fur-trading Company as and when required. This included not only his skills as an apothecary but a number of other duties besides the medical care of the inhabitants.

In 1621 the fur trade rights for New France had been conferred for a period of 11 years on Emery and Guillaume de Caën, Huguenot merchants of Rouen, by the Viceroy Momtmorency. On one occasion in the summer of 1622

Hébert was directed by Emery de Caën to go to Tadoussac with him. When he departed from Tadoussac, de Caën left Hébert in charge of his vessel that was moored there. This is an indication of a type of service that Hébert was required to perform, notwithstanding it was at a significant distance from his home and family.

Champlain subsequently wrote of an altercation involving Hébert which occurred while Louis was in command of de Caën's ship at Tadoussac. The incident involved seems rather frivolous today, but it provides an image of Hébert which indicates that he could be strong-willed when he felt it necessary.

Raymond de La Ralde, de Caën's lieutenant, arrived at Tadoussac and purported to take over control from Hébert. Hébert refused to acknowledge La Ralde's authority. A heated disagreement ensued between Hébert and La Ralde in relation to where the Roman Catholics and the Huguenots should say their prayers on the ship.

When de Caën was present, the Huguenots prayed in his cabin in the stern of the ship, while the Catholics did so in the bow. Hébert had followed this practice in de Caën's absence.

La Ralde (a Roman Catholic as was Hébert) decided that these places of prayer should be reversed with the Catholics in the cabin and the Huguenots in the bow. Hébert objected stating that de Caën did not intend this. The dispute could only be settled with the assistance of some Recollet priests and others who were present.

Although Champlain was not there, he somehow arrived at the conclusion that "Hébert was in the wrong in this quarrel, and was not reasonable about it."

Chapter Reference Sources

* *Backwoodswoman, The* by Isabel Skelton, chapter I, p. 21-22.
* *Champlain: The Life of Fortitude* by Morris Bishop, p. 234.
* *The Founder of New France: a Chronicle of Champlain, The* by Charles W. Colby in the *Chronicles of New France*, p. 81.
* "Hébert, Louis" by Ethel M. G. Bennett in the *Dictionary of Canadian Biography*, Vol. I, p. 367-368.

- *History of the Canadian People, A* by M. H. Long, Vol. 1, p. 235.
- *Louis Hébert - Premier Colon du Canada* by Laure Conan, p. 21-22.
- *Old Quebec - Trails and Homes* by E. C. Woodley, p. 16-17.
- *Pioneers of France in the New World* by Francis Parkman, Vol. 2, p. 251.
- *Works of Samuel de Champlain, The* general editor H. P. Biggar Vol. III, p. 205 and Vol. V, p. 85-86; 116.
- *White and the Gold - The French Regime in Canada, The* by Thomas B. Costain, p. 91.

Chapter XII

MOMENTOUS EVENTS FOR THE HÉBERTS

In his daily life in Quebec Louis Hébert was kept busy tending to his land with its crops of fruits, vegetables, herbs and grains. However, in his professional capacity he also looked after the medical ailments and disorders of the inhabitants of the trading fort, as well as those of the natives who came to him for help. In those days, particularly in that place, an apothecary also performed the functions of a physician.

This inter-action with the fur traders, carpenters, masons, aboriginals, and other workers included a young man from the fort named Étienne Jonquest (some sources spell his surname Jonquet or Jonquit). He had come to Quebec from Normandy. He may have come on the same ship that brought the Hébert family to Quebec.

It soon became clear that Jonquest had more on his mind than seeing the only apothecary/physician in the community in order to be treated or to receive medication. The Héberts eldest child Anne, who was in her teens, had obviously captured Étienne's eye.

In light of subsequent events, it is easy to visualize him being invited to the Hébert home on the summit for visits and dinner on a regular basis. It is not so easy to visualize how the young couple could have courted without avoiding prying eyes in such a small community. Perhaps they did so by taking walks in the nearby forest or along the river's edge.

In any event, court they did. The year following the Héberts' arrival in Quebec they were married. Historically, this was the first formal marriage of Europeans in a Canadian church. Gabriel Sagard wrote in his *Histoire du Canada* (published in Paris in 1636):

> Father Joseph performed the first marriage in Canada, between Étienne Jonquest of Normandy and Anne Hébert, oldest daughter of Louis Hébert, who had arrived

93

in Quebec the year before with his wife, two daughters and a son with the intention of residing there.

Sagard was a lay brother who came to New France on June 24, 1623 with the Recollets (a branch of the Roman Catholic Franciscan Order founded by St. Francis of Assisi in 1209). In 1632 after returning to Paris, Sagard also wrote *The Long Journey to the Country of the Hurons*. The two works of Sagard give details of the living habits and customs of the natives and describe the missionary activities of the Recollets.

The happiness with which the young Étienne and Anne felt on the joyous occasion of their wedding did not last long. The year after their marriage Anne died in childbirth, as did her newborn infant. Soon after, her husband Étienne also passed away. These deaths must have been very difficult for the Héberts, particularly seeing their teenage daughter taken from them on the threshold of her adult life.

However, life carried on. The officials of the merchant company that had the fur-trading monopoly did little to encourage Hébert in his farm activities. On the contrary, they remained quite dissatisfied with Hébert's efforts in this respect.

They made matters difficult for him, undoubtedly to signal that they wanted settlers to stay away from Quebec. According to Després they accused him of trading with the natives and forced him to surrender his surplus grain to the Company. Brother Sagard, indignant at the unfairness towards Hébert, wrote:

> Oh God! everywhere the big fish eat the little ones.

Hébert complained to Champlain about being hassled, but Champlain was unable to help him.

In 1618 Champlain wrote both the King and the Paris Chamber of Commerce seeking greater support for New France. In his correspondence to the King he emphasized the opportunities for the conversion of the natives by missionaries and for French expansion.

He indicated that he had been told by a great number of people how to reach China, the East Indies and their riches. He undertook to discover the South Sea passage to these exotic places via the St. Lawrence River.

He added that this would result in huge profits for the King in taxes and duties imposed on merchants using this much shorter passage to take their oriental goods back to Europe. Champlain further stated he would build a town and a temple at Quebec called *Ludovica* and that settlers would keep out the English and the Flemings.

He also said that he would need priests, families and missionaries. In this respect he stated that he would immediately bring 15 Recollet friars and 300 families to New France.

Champlain took a different tack with the Paris Chamber of Commerce. To entice their support he pointed out the great wealth that could be obtained for France from the fisheries, forests, mines, furs and other products. He itemized and calculated the annual value at an amazing 5,400,000 livres. As Morris Bishop in his biography of Champlain indicated, these calculations could not be taken seriously.

The Chamber did send Champlain's correspondence to the King, requesting funds for Champlain. The Chamber and everyone else other than Champlain promptly disregarded the whole affair. Furthermore the obstructive and unfriendly tactics of Champlain's employers positively discouraged colonization.

Although Champlain's principals had an obligation to colonize as a condition of their royal trading monopoly, they did little in this respect. In 1627, nine years after he wrote to the King and to the Paris Chamber of Commerce and 19 years after the establishment of the fort at Quebec, Champlain stated: "We were in all sixty-five souls, including men, women and children."

In the "The Works of Samuel de Champlain" edited by H. P. Biggar, there is a statement that:

> The only family that had established and maintained itself was
> that of the late Hébert.

Champlain added that it was with some difficulty that Hébert did so because the Company had compelled him to submit to a number of unlawful conditions.

It also required him to sell to the Company grains he raised at a price fixed by the Company. Champlain also noted that their object was to discourage settlers and to have complete control of the country.

In his book *The Long Journey to the Country of the Hurons*, Brother Gabriel Sagard in writing of the animosity of the associates of the fur-trading company to settlement in New France stated:

> .... the country is almost uninhabited and uncultivated
> .... through the negligence and lack of interest of the
> merchants ....

He added that they were unwilling to spend money in this respect as there interest was in furs and profit, not in cultivation and settlement.

Although Hébert was a gentleman, he clearly was fed up with the vexatious attitude and unfair dealings of the Company towards him. Hébert decided to fight back.

In 1621 when a proper legal system was being put into place, Hébert received the appointment of Royal Procurator in the first court of justice in Quebec. In this capacity he signed a petition on August 18 of that year to the King of France, Louis XIII, from the inhabitants of Quebec.

This undoubtedly was the first petition in Canadian history. The English version of the petition appears in the 1691 book *First Establishment of the Faith in New France* by Father Christian Le Clercq.

The petition protested the fur-trading company's monopoly and asked the King to end their abuses. It stated in part that a general assembly was held of all the inhabitants of New France to consider proper measures:

.... in regard to the ruin and desolation of all this country, and to seek the means of preserving the Catholic, Apostolic, and Roman religion intact.

It also referred to "the disorders", and the "imminent ruin of the whole country."

Besides that of Hébert, signatures on the petition included those of Father Joseph LeCaron, Pierre Desportes, Eustache Boullé, Olivier Letardif, Champlain, Pierre Reye, I. LeGroux, and Father Denis Jamay.

Father Georges Le Bailiff, a Recollet priest, was appointed the deputy of the inhabitants to present the petition to the Viceroy, the Duke of Montmorency. He was instructed to tell him of their complaints and to:

.... request a remedy to the many evils that threaten these lands with coming ruin.

Le Bailiff left for Paris on September 7, 1621. In a letter that he addressed to the King he gave a colorful picture of the lands, the fruits and the animals in the St. Lawrence River area. A translation of this letter appears in Father Le Clercq's book.

In his letter Father Le Bailiff described the St. Lawrence area as having:

many beautiful and fertile islands, stocked with such an abundance of all kinds of fish as can not be described, bordered by hills full of fruit trees such as walnuts, chestnuts, plums, cherries and wild vines, with numerous meadows which adorn and embellish the valleys .... peopled with all kinds of game .... besides elks .... beaver, black fox, and other animals, the fur of which gives access and hope of a very great trade hereafter. Moreover the fertility of this country has been more and more established ....

However, Father Le Bailiff was not the sterling individual his appointment might suggest. On January 13, 1622, while in Paris, he filed a complaint with the Council of State. In it he alleged that Louis Hébert in the service of the de Caëns had attacked him. There is no record of the outcome of this allegation. However, such an attack by Hébert would have been wholly out of character.

If, as Father Le Bailiff alleged, Hébert had punched him (which was probably a fabrication) perhaps he was pushed over the edge by the chicanery and duplicity of Father Le Bailiff.

Marcel Trudel wrote in *The Beginnings of New France* that about this time Le Bailiff had issued "a violent anonymous pamphlet". Guillaume de Caën and his associates were accused of various crimes in this pamphlet. It contained supporting evidence including counterfeit letters purporting to be written by Champlain and others. According to Trudel these letters:

> .... were pure fabrications.... Father Le Bailiff .... had turned out to be a forger.

Guillemette, the daughter of Louis Hébert and Marie Rollet, married Guillaume Couillard at Quebec on August 26, 1621. Couillard had arrived in Quebec in 1613 to work as a carpenter and shipwright for the Company of Canada. At the time of his marriage, this Company's monopoly had been turned over by the Viceroy, the Duke of Montmorency, to Guillaume de Caën and his nephew Emery. The de Caëns were Huguenot merchants of Rouen, France. A chapter later in this book discusses Guillaume Couillard and his wife Guillemette Hébert.

Because of the callous attitude of the merchant fur-trading company to settlers and land cultivation, Louis Hébert was apprehensive about not having ownership of the land that he had so laboriously developed. He was concerned that at some point he might be dispossessed of his home and lands.

Champlain was unable to aid him in obtaining title to his property. Since Hébert realized that Champlain had little or no influence in France in this respect, Hébert decided to take matters into his own hands.

He sent his own petition in 1622 directly to the Viceroy in Paris requesting title to his lands in Canada. On February 4, 1623 the Duke of Montmorency granted Hébert a concession giving him free and full possession of his lands.

The lands granted to Hébert were later designated as the fief Sault-au-Matelot. This was the first seigneurial grant of land in New France. Prior to the Company of New France being formed by Cardinal Richilieu in 1627, two additional seigneurial grants of land were made. These were Cap Tourmente to Guillaume de Caën in 1624, and Notre Dame des Anges to the Jesuits in 1626.

The latter seigneury became the foundation of the extensive landholding which many years later became known as the Jesuits' Estates. As a matter of interest, over two centuries later the Jesuits' Estates became the center of a political controversy in Quebec.

In 1888 the Jesuits' Estates Act was enacted by the Province of Quebec based on arbitration by Pope Leo XIII. Under this Act a monetary settlement was to be paid to the Jesuits and other institutions in Quebec. The Orange Order in Ontario was outraged at what they considered to be interference by the Papacy in Canada's affairs. A stormy debate ensued in the House of Commons to disallow the Act, but the vote to do so was emphatically defeated.

Two years after the seigneurial grant of 1623 to Louis Hébert, the Duke of Montmorency decided to give up his vice-regal position in charge of New France. He stated it was more trouble than being the Admiral of Old France, which he had been some years earlier. He was succeeded by his nephew Henri de Lévis, the Duke of Ventadour, a pious 29 year old.

Ventadour was more interested in converting the "infidels" of New France, i.e. the natives, than in trade or colonization. He felt that the Jesuits with their zeal and resources were most suitable for this purpose.

In the year that he was appointed, Ventadour paid the costs of sending six Jesuit priests to New France. Among them was Jean de Brébeuf who was tortured and martyred by the Iroquois in 1649 and was canonized in 1930. The organizer of this mission and the first Superior of the

Jesuits in Quebec was Charles Lalemant, who later became procurator of the missions to New France. His brother was Father Jérôme Lalemant who was also a Jesuit missionary in New France.

When Louis Hébert learned of Ventadour's becoming Viceroy, he wanted assurance that this would not affect the land title granted to him by the Duke of Montmorency. Again aware that Champlain would be of no help in this respect, Hébert personally petitioned Ventadour to ratify his land concession.

Not only did Ventadour uphold the grant, he confirmed that the lands were to be held by Hébert as a "noble fief". He went even further in that he acknowledged Hébert's services to the colony.

By a formal agreement dated the last day of February 1626, signed and sealed by Ventadour and countersigned by Girardet, Hébert's concession was confirmed. In addition Hébert was granted a further noble fief consisting of a French league of land adjacent to the St. Charles River.

As a result of these grants of noble fiefs by the Viceroy, Louis Hébert became the first nobleman, or seigneur, in New France. The land along the St. Charles River was originally called the fief St. Joseph carrying with it the title of Sieur d' Espinay. Subsequently that land was known as the fief de Lespinay.

The document containing Ventadour's ratification and new grant of additional land to Hébert sets forth in some details the unique contributions which Hébert made to the first colonization of New France. In this document the fiefdoms were granted to Hébert and his successors and heirs in perpetuity. An English translation of this document is set forth as Appendix "A" to this book.

Abbé Déprés in his other book *La Première Famille Française au Canada* writes that the fief Sault-au-Matelot remained the property of the Couillard family until 1663. After the death of her husband Guillaume Couillard in that year, Guillemette Couillard (the daughter of Louis Hébert) sold the lands of the Haute-Ville (Upper Town) to

Monsignor de Laval. This land was used by Laval for the establishment of the Quebec Minor Seminary.

As the year 1626 came to a close, Hébert was more than secure in his land holdings. He was now a nobleman, a seigneur. He was held in high esteem by the community for:

- his pioneering efforts in establishing the first single permanent family household by a European in what is now Canada;

- clearing the land, sowing crops, developing a vineyard, and planting a garden; and

- ministering to the medical needs of the fur trading post and the natives.

From his earliest arrival in Acadia in 1604, Hébert had consulted with the natives in order to learn about the herbal remedies and medical procedures of the natives. He integrated their traditional folk medicine with his European knowledge and training. In New France he combined his services as a pharmacist with that of a physician, which was then not unusual. He treated aboriginal people as well as the staff of the fort.

He had a family that loved and revered him. He had two lovely granddaughters. In January 1625 he had become a grandfather when his daughter Guillemette and her husband Guillaume Couillard had a baby girl named Louise. In August of the following year Marguerite, another granddaughter and sister for Louise, was born.

His son-in-law Guillaume Couillard had also become a farmer and a permanent settler. Life must have seemed happy and fulfilling for him after the many trials he had endured earlier on.

Louis Hébert undoubtedly felt that he had many more years of happiness and prosperity with his wife and family in his adopted homeland of New France. Sadly, his hopes and endeavors for an even brighter future were brought to an end by his untimely death a short time later.

Chapter Reference Sources

- *Beginnings of New France, The* by Marcel Trudel, p. 131-32; 139.
- *Canadian Frontier, 1534-1760, The* by W. J. Eccles, p. 32.
- *Champlain: The Life of Fortitude* by Morris Bishop, p. 48; 235-37; 256-57.
- *Documents Relating to The Seigniorial Tenure in Canada* edited by William Bennett Munro, p. xxiv; 4.
- *First Establishment of the Faith in New France* by Father Christian Le Clercq, p. 164-73.
- *Founder of New France: a Chronicle of Champlain, The* by Charles W. Colby, p. 81.
- "Hébert, Louis" by Ethel M. G. Bennett in *Dictionary of Canadian Biography*, Vol. I, p. 367-368.
- *Histoire de la Nouvelle France* by Marcel Trudel, Vol. II, p. 260; 263.
- *Histoire du Canada* by Brother Gabriel Sagard, p. 41.
- *Jesuit Relations* by Father Charles Lalemant, Vol. IV, p. 271.
- *La Première Famille Française au Canada* by Abbé Azarie Couillard Després, p. 64-65; 78.
- *Long Journey to the Country of the Hurons, The*, Brother Gabriel Sagard, p. 52-53.
- "Louis Hébert" by M. Charlton in the *John Hopkins Hospital Bulletin*, Vol. 25, No. 279, May 1914, p. 158-160.
- *Louis Hébert - Premier Colon Canadien et sa Famille* by Abbé Azarie Couillard Després, *passim*.
- *Old Quebec - Trails and Homes* by E.C. Woodley, p. 17-20.
- *Romance of Quebec, The* by J. C. Sutherland, p. 44-48.
- "*Samuel de Champlain - Father of New France*" by Samuel Eliot Morison, p. 171-73.
- *White and the Gold - The French Regime in Canada, The* by Thomas B. Costain, p. 89-92.
- *Works of Samuel de Champlain, The* general editor H. P. Biggar, Vol. V, p. 326-27.

Chapter XIII

DEATH OF LOUIS HÉBERT

The winter of 1626 came early to Quebec. The snow was almost five feet deep. There was ice in numerous places. On a wintry day, Louis Hébert had a serious accident when he slipped and smashed his head on the ice. Although he clung to life for a short time, he succumbed to his injuries on January 25, 1627. The small community was shocked.

The beloved first habitant and first apothecary of New France, who had served one and all in the community, was dead. Hébert's wife and family were heartbroken to see their patriarch snatched from them so suddenly.

There was dismay and sadness that extended beyond the community to the natives. Hébert had always treated the natives with decency and respect, and had accepted them as intelligent human beings.

Prior to his death Hébert received from Father Joseph Le Caron the sacraments of the Roman Catholic Church. These were the Holy Viaticum (the Eucharist given to a person near death) and Extreme Unction (the anointing with oil of one near death).

On his death bed Hébert gave a touching exhortation. Abbé Després quotes Brother Sagard about Hébert's moving final words. Sagard wrote that Hébert's life religiously corresponded to that of a true Christian and that he was a man without artificiality or cunning.

Sagard stated that as he was dying Hébert drew his wife and family near to his bed. He talked to them on the vanity of this life, on the treasures of heaven, and on the merit which one will obtain from God in working for the salvation of others. According to Sagard Hébert said:

> I die content since Our Father has been pleased to give me the grace of seeing the uncivilized [natives] die who had been converted. I crossed the seas to come and help them, rather than for any private interest, and I gladly die for their conversion if such is the good pleasure of God. I beseech you to love them as I have loved them,

and to assist them according to your ability. God wishes you to do so and you will be rewarded in Paradise. They are responsible creatures like us, and they could love the same God as us if they become knowledgeable about Him, and to this goal I implore you to assist them by your examples and your prayers.

I also exhort you to peace, and to maternal and filial love, that you yourselves be respectful of one another, for in this you comply with the law of God, founded on charity.

This life is of short duration, and after this comes eternity. I am ready to go before my God, who is my judge, to whom I must render an account of all my past life. Pray to Him for me, so that I may finally find grace before His face, and that I may one day be of his chosen people.

"Then" as set forth in Després' book, Sagard continued:

.... raising his hand he gave all of them his blessing, and gave up his spirit into the arms of his Creator on the 25th day of January, 1627, the day of the conversion of St. Paul.

Undoubtedly the tears of Hébert's family must have flowed like the River Jordan during his inspiring deathbed words and when he passed away.

Over 60 years after his death, a tribute to Hébert was written in 1691 by Father Christian Le Clercq, a Recollet priest. At the time of writing this tribute, Le Clercq was not a witness to the events but was writing the history of the *First Establishment of the Faith in New France.*

However, when he arrived in New France in 1670 there were still people alive from whom he would have received first-hand information on the death of Louis Hébert. For instance Le Clercq writes in two places of conversations he had with Guillemette Couillard (nee Hébert) stating:

She was still alive when I was in Canada.

As well Le Clercq was in Quebec in 1678, the year in which the body of Louis Hébert was re-interred in the

Recollet Cemetery amidst a public show of admiration. The following is the tribute to Hébert that Le Clercq wrote:

> We had at this time another grief. Monsieur Hébert, the first settler of the colony, of whom we have spoken in the beginning of this history, fell sick .... and, after lingering some days, he paid the debt of nature. His death was universally regretted. He may be called the Abraham of the colony, the father of the living and the faithful, since his posterity has become as numerous as we have heretofore said.

In the six volumes of *The Works of Samuel de Champlain* the only reference which Champlain made to the death of Hébert, his long-time acquaintance in Acadia and Quebec, was the following:

> On the 25th day of January Hébert had a fall which caused his death. He was the first head of a family resident in the country who lived on the produce of his land.

On the other hand Le Clercq recognized Champlain's immense contribution in inviting Hébert to come to Canada when Le Clercq wrote:

> .... the most fortunate thing he [Champlain] effected was his persuading Sieur Hébert to go to Canada with all his family, which has produced, and will hereafter produce, good subjects, the most important and zealous in the colony.

John G. Shea, the translator of Le Clercq's work, made the following personal observation concerning the contribution that Hébert made to New France:

> Louis Hébert, apothecary, is regarded as the father of Canada.

In *The Romance of Quebec*, J. C. Sutherland wrote:

> The story of Louis Hébert, the first real settler and the first farmer of Canada, is a simple one, but it is one that is cherished in Quebec to this day. Here was a family of courageous and noble character, who faced toil and difficulties innumerable, who lived to see the success of their endeavours, and who left long generations to honour them and follow their example.

Louis Hébert's funeral was very solemn. Almost the entire population of the community was present. It was looked upon as a public funeral.

Hébert was buried amidst much sorrow in the Quebec cemetery of the Recollet Fathers. There has been conjecture that Hébert may have had a premonition of his death. Only a few days before his accident he had visited the Recollets. At that time he expressed to the Father Superior a desire to be interred at the foot of the great cross in their cemetery.

In 1678 a massive landslide occurred in the cemetery. Hébert's coffin, made of cedar wood and containing his remains, was exhumed and carried to the vault of the chapel of the church that had been recently built by the Recollets.

Father Le Clercq wrote that:

.... the body of him [Hébert] who had been the stock of the inhabitants of the country is the first whose bones rest in that vault.

Hébert's daughter Guillemette Couillard, then in her seventies, participated in the event. Le Clercq wrote that Guillemette was carried there to witness the re-interment of her father's body. Notwithstanding the passage of time since Hébert's death over 50 years earlier, the conveyance of the coffin was marked by a great public demonstration. The memory of Louis Hébert had remained strong.

In his 1908 book *Canadian Types of the Old Regime: 1608-1698* McGill University history professor Charles W. Colby stated that some of the best-known Canadian families are descended from Louis Hébert. Some of the names he mentioned were:

Joliet, De Téry, De Ramezay, D'Eschambeault, and Fornier. Mgr. Taschereau, Mgr. Taché, and Archbishop Blanchet are also among his descendants.

Mgr. Taché mentioned by Colby was Archbishop A.A. Taché who in the 19th century moved from Quebec to the Red River Settlement. He was in charge of the Catholic

Church in Western Canada during some of the most momentous events in Canadian history.

Some of Hébert's other direct descendants became voyageurs and fur traders in what is now Western Canada. Among them was Jacques Goulet, the great-great grandfather of the author George Goulet. Jacques married a Metis woman from the Saskatchewan area. One grandson of Jacques was Elzear Goulet, the Metis martyr who was stoned to death for his involvement in the Red River Resistance of 1869-70.

Chapter Reference Sources

* *Canadian Types of the Old Regime: 1608-1698* by Charles W. Colby, p. 125; 129-31.
* *Champlain: The Life of Fortitude* by Morris Bishop, p. 261.
* *First Establishment of the Faith in New France* by Father Christian Le Clercq p. 115; 155; 180; 280-81.
* "Hébert', Louis" by Ethel M. G. Bennett in *The Dictionary of Canadian Biography* Vol. I, p. 367-68.
* "Le Clercq, Chrestien [Christian]" by G. M. Dumas in *The Dictionary of Canadian Biography*, Vol. I, p. 438-41.
* *Louis Hébert: Premier Colon Canadien et sa Famille* by Abbé Azarie Couillard Després, p. 65; 68; 70-72.
* *Louis Hébert* by Julia Jarvis, p. 21-22.
* Louis Hébert" by M. Charlton in the *Johns Hopkins Hospital Bulletin*, Vol. 25, p. 158-60.
* *Romance of Quebec, The* by J. C. Sutherland, p. 47-48.
* *Works of Samuel de Champlain, The* general editor H. P. Biggar, Vol. V, p. 212.

SECTION C

MARIE ROLLET

PIONEER HOMEMAKER, TEACHER,

AND FIRST FEMALE COLONIAL SETTLER

Madame Hébert - Marie Rollet
by Charles W. Jefferys

Marie Rollet

by P. Monnin

Chapter XIV

CANADA'S FIRST PIONEER WOMAN

There is a pen and ink drawing by the noted Canadian historical artist, Charles W. Jefferys, depicting a lone woman on the heights of Quebec overlooking the Habitation and the wharf at the foot of the cliff on which she is standing. She is witnessing the departure of a ship in the St. Lawrence River. Beyond the River to the north and the east stretch the Beauport shore and the Laurentian hills.

The lady in the drawing is dressed like a pioneer woman of the period. She is wearing a heavy skirt down to her ankles, a short jacket, an apron, and wooden shoes. A scarf is wrapped around her head and shoulders, and she is holding it together with her right hand. In her left hand she clutches a mattock, a type of pickaxe used to break up the soil.

The ship depicted is the English one commanded by David Kirke. It was carrying as prisoners most of the French inhabitants of Quebec, including Champlain and Pontgravé, back to Europe. The correct year of the event represented in the drawing is 1629.

The caption, under this creative drawing, states:

Madame Hébert watching the departure of the French from Quebec after its capture 1628 [sic].

Madame Hébert is, of course, Marie Rollet. This picture symbolizes the courage, the hardiness, the perseverance, the determination, and the love of Canada of this extraordinary trail-blazing woman.

Marie Rollet's heart must have ached to see the exodus of so many of her friends and acquaintances that she had made over the years in New France. However her resolve to remain in the adopted homeland that she cherished was unshakeable.

In addition, Marie Rollet had to bear the heartbreaking pain of the premature death of her beloved husband, partner and the father of her children. She was the first

European woman to come to Canada with her family for the specific purpose of living there permanently. She was a faithful wife and a loving mother and grandmother.

Marie Rollet was extremely brave in electing to stay in New France after it was conquered by the English in 1629. After consulting with Champlain she nevertheless made that decision knowing that he, Pontgravé, all of the Jesuit and Recollet priests, and most of the community (except for a few other families), were leaving for France.

However the English quickly came to respect and like her. Her home was always open to all. As J. E. Wetherell wrote:

> She spent the three years under the rule of the English as she had spent the earlier years under French rule - in hard work, in doing all manner of services for others, and in a life of piety, although cut off from the benefits of her church.

Her home, the first in New France constructed by Europeans as a permanent private family residence, was like a sanctuary. It welcomed the clergy, the children, the natives, and the people from the fort. This hospitality reflected her warm and friendly personality.

An observer of the events of this time, Father LeJeune wrote of her:

> She has a beautiful family. Her daughter is married to an upright Frenchman here. God blesses them every day. He has given them very beautiful children, their cattle are flourishing, their lands yield fine grain. This is the only French family settled in Canada ....

Marie Rollet was born in France in the 1580s, likely in Paris. She married Louis Hébert around 1601. As previously noted they had three children, all born in France. The oldest was Anne, followed by another daughter about 1606 who they named Guillemette. Their son Guillaume was their youngest child.

Marie's first trip to the New World was to Port Royal, Acadia in 1610. Maude Abbott wrote the following concerning the time that Marie spent in Acadia:

.... during the years from 1610 to 1613 [Hébert] was again at Port Royal, this time accompanied by his wife, who was thus the first [non-native] woman to set foot on Canadian sod.

In her monograph titled *Louis Hébert* the author Julia Jarvis wrote that:

Madame de Poutrincourt and Marie Rollet, Hébert's young wife, were the first two women to settle in New France.

Madame de Poutrincourt was Louis Hébert's first cousin. Jarvis added that the following spring, after a winter of great suffering, the Sieur de Poutrincourt took his wife back to France.

She also noted that:

Madame Hébert loved the country no less than her brave husband.... They lived happily and comfortably in Port Royal until the year 1613.

In that year the settlement was captured and burned by "an English buccaneer" i.e. Samuel Argall. The Héberts then returned to France where Louis reopened his apothecary shop.

As noted earlier, a memorable change occurred in 1617 for Marie, her husband Louis and their three children when they made a life-altering decision to move to Quebec. Hébert was practicing his profession in Paris when Champlain invited him to come with him to Quebec. Champlain's main reason was to obtain the services of an apothecary, who could also act as a physician, for the employees of the fur trading post.

After considering the persuasive and favorable proposal presented by Champlain, Hébert decided to accept the offer on condition that he would be able to bring his family with him.

After disposing of his business and their assets, the Hébert family set out for the Port of Honfleur on the west coast of France. The distressing events prior to their embarkation, the dreadful and near-calamitous ocean crossing, and their settling down in Quebec have been recounted in earlier chapters of this book.

Their departure for Quebec was the last time that they would see France or set foot on its soil. Marie Rollet, her husband and children were destined to live the rest of their lives in their new homeland of Canada.

Louis Hébert and Marie Rollet brought with them to Quebec their three children who had been born in France. Their two daughters were Anne and Guillemette, and their only son was name Guillaume.

Anne, the eldest daughter, died in 1619 in childbirth as did her newborn child. She had been married the year before to Étienne Jonquest.

Guillemette married Guillaume Couillard and they had ten children. A subsequent chapter in this book provides more information concerning the Couillard family.

Guillaume Hébert married Hélène Desportes. They had only one son Joseph who was born on November 3, 1636. Joseph was the only grandson of Marie Rollet and Louis Hébert who bore the Hébert name. Joseph was killed by Iroquois Indians in June 1661, and his only son died in infancy the same year. His father Guillaume had predeceased him in 1639.

All the grandchildren of Marie and Louis were to be born and live their entire lives in Canada. One of them Elizabeth Couillard was born at Quebec on February 9, 1631 during its occupation by the British forces. Two others, Louise born in 1625 and Marguerite born in 1626 (children of Guillaume and Guillemette Couillard) were born before their grandfather Louis Hébert died in 1627.

Today, there are many persons who trace their direct lineage to Louis Hébert and Marie Rollet. However after the deaths in the 1660s of their only grandson and great grandson bearing the Hébert surname, they had no further descendants that inherited the Hébert surname.

All through her life Marie Rollet was a fine and industrious homemaker. The following is a translation of a passage written by Laure Conan in 1912 about Marie moving into her new stone home on the Quebec heights:

> On that day, the furnishings brought from Paris were arranged. One could forget that they were living right in the middle of a savage land in a forest without bounds.... With a quick and merry eye Madame Hébert went to and fro placing the furniture, arranging the linen in the armoires, setting the beautiful plates and dishes of pewter on the sideboard and the copper pots near the fire.

In 1913 Abbé Couillard Després wrote that one could see, at the Quebec Monastery of the Sisters of the Good Shepherd, an antique fountain that was brought to Canada by Louis Hébert. He said that it had been preserved by the Couillard family from generation to generation.

Isabel Skelton wrote a book on a number of heroic women in the building up of Canada titled *The Backwoodswoman*. The book refers to:

> .... the women who in the early years of the colony carried on staunchly and heroically day after day under conditions which would make people of today quail even to think of them.

The first chapter of her book is titled "Marie Hébert: the First Woman Settler in Canada". In this chapter, Skelton recounts the instructions of de Monts to Champlain in 1608. These included establishing a fur-trading warehouse and habitation in New France, and the selection of the site for Quebec.

Skelton also wrote about the appeal by Champlain to Louis Hébert to come to Quebec and that Champlain had remembered Hébert from the first trading post at St. Croix that de Monts had established in 1604 where the ".... most efficient helper had been Louis Hébert."

Louis Hébert had subsequently returned to France. This was in 1607 when de Monts' Royal monopoly was revoked. In 1610 Hébert sailed again for Port Royal with his wife Marie Rollet.

Skelton then added that:

It was on the practical, solid, sterling work of Louis Hébert and his wife Marie that Champlain's hopes for the future of New France were builded [sic].

In their early Quebec days Louis and Marie were sometimes separated for many days at a time. Skelton writes that Marie's:

.... husband, in accordance with his agreement, was away most of the time superintending the Fur Company's trade at Tadoussac, or taking charge of their boats down the river.

Marie must have been devastated by the death of her husband, Louis Hébert, on January 25, 1627. However she had the consolation of knowing that her children and two infant grandchildren were with her at this sad time.

She carried on with her activities after her husband's sudden death. Some months after Marie was widowed, the baptism of a young native boy took place.

The missionaries wanted to impress the natives with the ceremony, no doubt in an attempt to encourage further native baptisms. The lad, dressed all in white, was presented at the church, responded to the solemn ritual questions and was baptized.

His godfather and godmother were the most prominent man and woman in Quebec at that time. They were Samuel Champlain and Marie Rollet. A hymn praising God was sung by all.

It was accompanied by the firing of the fort's cannons, signaling the admission of a new member to the church. After the christening Marie Rollet hosted a large crowd, including many natives, to a huge banquet in her home.

Abbé Després wrote that she served at this feast 56 bustards (probably geese or wild turkey), 30 ducks, 20 teals, a large amount of meats, two barrels of peas, a barrel of galettes (ship's biscuits), 15 to 20 pounds of plums, and Indian corn. No doubt she was assisted in the preparation of this feast by her family and possibly other ladies from the community.

In October 1627, two of the French cowhands at Cap Tourmente were murdered by one of the Montagnais natives. The killer fled to avoid the wrath of the French. Champlain addressed a meeting of the Montagnais natives about this matter. Champlain took the killer's child as a prisoner until the murderer returned to face justice.

Le Clercq wrote of this incident that the Frenchmen were axed to death because an:

> .... Indian had been ill-treated by Madame Hébert's baker and by another whom he asked for bread, perhaps too importunately.

In his biography of Champlain, N. E. Dionne in referring to these murders indicated that:

> .... one named Dumoulin and the other Henri, a servant of the widow Hébert were found dead.

Dionne further wrote that they had been shot, thus differing from Le Clercq's version of the manner of their death. Henri was the faithful servant of the Hébert family who had come with them to Quebec in 1617. His death would have greatly saddened Marie Rollet.

Chapter Reference Sources

- *Backwoodswoman, The* by Isabel Skelton, chapter I.
- *Champlain - Founder of Quebec, Father of New France* by N. E. Dionne, p. 164.
- *Champlain: The Life of Fortitude* by Morris Bishop, (McClelland and Stewart Limited, Toronto, 1963), p. 264.
- *First Establishment of the Faith in New France* by Father Christian Le Clercq, p. 282-83.
- "Hébert, Louis" by Ethel M. G. Bennett in the *Dictionary of Canadian Biography* Vol. I, p. 367.
- *History of Medicine in the Province of Quebec* by Maude Abbott, p. 15.
- *History of the Canadian People, A* by M. H. Long, Vol. 1, p. 128.
- *Jesuit Relations* by Father Paul Le Jeune, Vol. V, p. 41-43.
- *Louis Hébert* by Julia Jarvis, p. 3; 13-14.
- *Louis Hébert - Premier Colon du Canada* by Laure Conan, p. 21-22.

- *Louis Hébert - Premier Colon Canadien et sa Famille* by Abbé Azarie Couillard Després, p. 49 (note 1), 99-100, 104-105.
- *Picture Gallery of Canadian History, The* by C. W. Jefferys, Vol. 1, p. 97.
- "Rollet, Marie" by Ethel M. G. Bennett in the *Dictionary of Canadian Biography* Vol. I, p. 578.
- *Three Centuries of Canadian Story* by J. E. Wetherell, p. 118-121.

Chapter XV

SURRENDER OF QUEBEC TO THE ENGLISH

After Hébert's death in 1627 life had carried on as usual at Quebec; however the fur trading fort was always dependent on supply ships from France arriving every summer to sustain and carry it through the ensuing winter.

Champlain's wife Hélène, whom he had married in 1610 when she was 12 years old, had abandoned Quebec in 1624 to return to the social life of Paris. He and Hélène had agreed that their relationship would now be that of brother and sister.

Champlain subsequently spent the winters of 1627, 1628 and 1629 in Quebec. This was contrary to his oft-repeated practice of returning to Paris to spend the winter months.

Being on site in Quebec during the summer of 1627, Champlain was concerned about the inadequacy of supplies. Word that relations between France and England had deteriorated also made him apprehensive about the security of the fort. Each country was commandeering ships of the other.

The winter of 1627-28 in Quebec was long and frigid, and hunting for moose and other wildlife was difficult. As well, many natives were practically without food and on the verge of starvation. A number of them came to Champlain pleading for food. He acceded to their request notwithstanding the meager provisions at the fort.

In return for his help, the natives gave him a gift of three girls, one a 15 year-old and the others 11 and 12 years old respectively. He accepted them and named them Faith, Hope and Charity. He was then 61 years old and, being childless himself, it is said that he treated them as if they were his children.

Because of the impending dire straits at the fort, Champlain decided to have a pinnace (a small boat) built with a view to sending some of the people from the fort to Gaspé to look for French fishing boats. Champlain approached Guillaume Couillard (Louis Hébert's son-in-law) to help.

Champlain considered Couillard the most skillful and able-bodied man and referred to him as "a good sailor, carpenter and caulker". Champlain asked Couillard to travel to Tadoussac to fit out the pinnace there. Couillard said that he would willingly fix up a couple of boats at their fort, but refused to go to Tadoussac. He was afraid of being murdered by natives and did not want to leave his wife and two babies alone.

Champlain threatened him with imprisonment, but Couillard remained adamant. He had no intention of risking his life and leaving his wife widowed with two fatherless infants.

Champlain then consulted with François du Pontgravé. They decided not to press the matter, but did ask Couillard to caulk two boats.

By the summer of 1628, conditions in Quebec were not looking good. On July 9th in calm weather and for no apparent reason two small towers at the fort collapsed. Some deemed this phenomenon to forebode a dismal future. The food supply was rapidly being depleted.

The inhabitants looked anxiously for the sails of ships from France in order that their stores might be replenished. Instead they learned that English vessels, ready for war, had arrived in the area of the Gaspé Peninsula under the command of David Kirke. His brothers Lewis and Thomas were with him.

Later that month, Nicolas Pivert arrived at the fort in a shallop (a light boat) with some Basque people. Pivert had been at Cap Tourmente some 30 miles down river tending crops and feeding cattle.

Champlain was told that the Kirkes had arrived at Cap Tourmente and destroyed the crops and the cattle, and overturned their chapel. After doing so, David Kirke had ordered Pivert and his group to take a letter to Champlain that demanded the surrender of Quebec.

Champlain knew that the fort was indefensible, but with the advice of Pontgravé and others he decided to bluff. He sent a reply to Kirke stating that they would "fight to the death". The Kirkes decided that rather than attack they would starve the fort into submission by blockading and engaging any supply ships sent out from France. They successfully did so, as noted hereafter.

David Kirke, then aged 32, carried letters of marque issued by Charles I of England to David's father Jarvis (or Gervase) Kirke in the spring of 1628. Letters of marque amounted to a royal license to commit acts of reprisal and seizure against an enemy. These acts would otherwise be considered piracy. The Kirke brothers acting under their father's letters of marque were privateers. Charles I also issued letters of marque to other privateers.

The background to the Kirke expedition down the St. Lawrence River involved hostilities between France and England. Among other matters, these nations were attacking each others ships. Although Charles I was married to Henrietta Maria, the Roman Catholic sister of Louis XIII (the reigning King of France), he gave encouragement to the French Huguenots and he prohibited the practice of Roman Catholicism in England.

Charles I was the King of England from 1625 to 1649. During his reign the English Civil War broke out. His Royalist forces, the Cavaliers, were defeated in 1648 by the puritanical Oliver Cromwell's Parliamentary forces, the Roundheads. Charles was tried, convicted and decapitated the following year. Thomas and Lewis Kirke fought for the Royalist Cavaliers in the Civil War and Thomas died in action.

In 1628 while en route to Quebec, David Kirke's ships accosted the vessels containing supplies for the fort. This shipment of supplies had been sent from France by the Company of New France. The Kirkes routed the supply ships.

The Company of New France, also called the Company of One Hundred Associates (the number of its subscribers), had been created by French royal decree the year before on April 29, 1627.

The influential Cardinal Richilieu had provided the initiative for the formation of this Company. He annulled the prior existing monopoly and saw to it that only Catholics were allowed to be subscribers to the new Company.

The Company of One Hundred Associates was granted all the lands to which France laid claim in the New World, including the lands of New France. The grant presumptuously encompassed an expansive area:

> .... from the coasts of Florida to the Arctic Circle, and from Newfoundland westward to the great lake commonly called the fresh sea [Lake Huron].

The Company was given a monopoly for a period of 15 years over all commerce including the fur trade. The fisheries were excluded from this grant. The Company also had an obligation to bring at least 200 settlers to New France in the first year and a total of 4,000 by the year 1643.

Richelieu also required that all settlers must be Roman Catholics - no Huguenots were allowed. Champlain was one of the associates of the Company as were members of the nobility, affluent merchants and small traders. To aid in raising capital, the Company was authorized to grant 12 titles of nobility.

In 1628, the year after its formation, the Company dispatched four vessels to New France under the command of Sieur Claude de Roquemont. These ships, accompanied by over a dozen fishing boats, carried extensive supplies for the fort and 200 potential settlers. However in the Gaspé near Tadoussac, this was the fleet that encountered the Kirkes.

A battle ensued, David Kirke's forces prevailed, Roquemont surrendered. Kirke torched some of the French vessels and took many prisoners. The Company of New France saw its ships and their contents forfeited to the

English, which was a crushing blow to the Company both financially and otherwise.

However before capitulating, Roquemont was able to have a shallop with 11 men slip away to Quebec. This was in early August 1628. These men told Champlain that they had fled from the battle scene and did not know its outcome. They also informed him of the formation of the Company of One Hundred Associates and its colonization objectives, and of the fleet sent out by Roquemont.

Champlain despaired at the news of the battle and the loss of supplies for the fort. He realized that the Kirkes, who had come to New France prepared for combat, would win the day. Instead of succor, he now had to split the fort's already skimpy rations among 11 additional mouths.

After defeating Roquemont, David Kirke remained until he was satisfied that no further ships were coming from France with supplies for Quebec. He and his fleet then sailed for England with many prisoners. However, the Kirke's were determined to return the following year in order to capture Quebec.

Not being vanquished by the Kirkes in 1628 was a mixed blessing for Champlain and the fort. It led to near starvation that winter and the following spring. Since there were close to 100 people to feed, Champlain apportioned the food and sent men to hunt. When they killed a moose, the hunters "devoured it like ravenous wolves" and brought very little back to the fort.

Champlain later wrote that he had waited for:

.... the harvest of peas and other grains on the cleared lands of the widow Hébert and her son-in-law [Guillaume Couillard], who had between them six and seven arpents sown....

This contemporary report by Champlain accords with the statement in the "Canadian Oxford Dictionary" that Marie Rollet:

.... was the first Frenchwoman to cultivate the soil of New France.

As winter wore on the people ate peas, roots, and acorns. Le Clercq wrote that:

> Dame Hébert [the widow of Louis] aided them with two barrels of peas.

The natives brought them eels but demanded a high price - one beaver pelt for each 10 eels. Men in a weakened state had to walk more than a mile in the snow to chop down trees for firewood. They then had to haul it back to the fort or else the inhabitants would have to live in frigid conditions.

Champlain later wrote that at this miserable time he had expected that the land of "Hébert and his son-in-law" (presumably Guillaume Couillard) would provide them with some of their harvested grain. Champlain further wrote that "they" indicated that this expectation was a reasonable one. However, Champlain said that all they could provide was a weekly basin of barley, peas and Indian corn weighing about nine and a half ounces. Champlain then wrote:

> Hébert [sic] did nothing by which we might know the amount he was grinding for himself, so as not to give cause for complaint that he was having better fare than the rest of us.

The reference to "Hébert" and "they" and "son-in-law" in these quotes is very bewildering. Louis Hébert had died in January 1627 (over one and one-half years prior to the events that Champlain was writing about). The only male Hébert was Marie Rollet's 15 year old son Guillaume. The teen-aged Guillaume Hébert was, of course, not old enough to have a "son-in-law" at the time of this incident.

Champlain implied selfishness on whomever he intended in his writings by adding that he trusted "them to gather their own crops", but that in times of need everyone tends to look after themselves. By his confusing Hébert reference, Champlain may have besmirched the name of Louis Hébert in the eyes of his readers in France who might not have known of Hébert's death many months before.

As for the Jesuits who had crops on their land, Champlain was more generous and less suspicious in his comments about them. This was so notwithstanding that they had provided no assistance whatsoever to the fort. Champlain wrote that the Jesuits only had enough to serve themselves and their 12 servants. He added that as a result they:

.... were unable to aid us, as I am sure they would have been glad to do.

By the spring of 1629 the fort was in a desperate situation due to the lack of food. In his overwhelming concern to provide food for the fort, Champlain contemplated having his malnourished men attack the Iroquois in order to get corn. However, he dismissed this idea.

Champlain sent some men to the Gaspé to look for help. They returned about the middle of June and reported that they had sighted a number of English ships in the area. They were six ships and two pinnaces under the command of David Kirke that had sailed from Gravesend, England on April 5, 1629.

A few weeks later Kirke's ships flying the English flag appeared at Quebec. A small boat displaying a white flag was dispatched and "an English gentleman", as Champlain dubbed him, set foot on the shore near the fort.

This Englishman went to Champlain and courteously handed him a letter on July 19, 1629 signed by Captain Lewis Kirke and Vice-Admiral Thomas Kirke. The letter stated that, pursuant to what their brother David had previously written to him the year before, Champlain could be assured of their friendship. The letter added that they were aware of the extreme destitution at the fort. It called upon Champlain to turn over the fort and Habitation to them.

Champlain did not reveal how desperate their situation was. He consulted the principal persons at the fort, including Pontgravé. Champlain then sent a reply asking for time to prepare terms under which he would surrender.

The Articles of Capitulation (also dated July 19, 1629) were signed by Champlain and Pontgravé.

In the Articles they requested that:

- the Kirkes show their commission from the King of England authorizing the seizure of the fort;

- a vessel be assigned to convey all of the inhabitants, including the priests and the two native girls Hope and Charity, to France (no mention was made of the older native girl Faith who had not remained with Champlain but had previously returned to her own people);

- they be permitted to take their personal possessions and arms;

- they be supplied with provisions for their journey back to France in exchange for furs; and

- the English refrain from any violence against them.

Most of these terms were agreed to by the Kirkes. However they would not accede to a separate vessel but instead assured the French of passage to England and from there to France. Champlain's request for the two young native girls to accompany them was refused.

Champlain subsequently met with Lewis Kirke. According to Champlain's account, he appealed to Kirke to provide soldiers to prevent the ransacking of the chapel and property of the priests and the homes of Marie Rollet (the widow of Louis Hébert) and her son-in-law and daughter Guillaume and Guillemette Couillard. Kirke agreed to do so.

Champlain was appalled to see that among the English were three French turncoats. They were Nicolas Marsolet, Etienne Brûlé and Pierre Reye. Marsolet had come with him to Quebec in 1608. Champlain wrote that though they called themselves Catholics these men had no objection to eating meat on Friday.

The English took control of the fort with 150 armed men on July 20, 1629. Champlain then talked Lewis Kirke into letting him take Hope and Charity (the two young native girls) with him to France. He impressed on Kirke that he had taught them religion and plain and fancy needlework. He also told Lewis that they were highly civilized and had an intense desire to go to France.

However David Kirke subsequently vetoed the idea. Consequently the Couillards assumed the care of the two native girls.

As for the Couillards and Marie Rollet, the widow of Louis Hébert, they decided to remain in Quebec rather than to return to France with Champlain and his party. A discussion in this respect appears in a subsequent chapter of this book.

According to Champlain in his writings, there was an incident involving Guillaume Couillard during the time the Kirkes occupied the fort. On June 26, 1629 (prior to the Kirkes' capturing the fort), Champlain had sent a pinnace with 30 men aboard up the St. Lawrence River under the command of his brother-in-law Eustache Boullé.

Champlain had told Boullé to try and find a French fishing vessel at the Gaspé or elsewhere to give them assistance or else to take the men to France. However, Boullé was captured by the Kirkes.

Before he was captured, Boullé encountered a ship commanded by Emery de Caën who told him that he had been sent from France by his uncle Guillaume de Caën for two reasons. One was to obtain any beaver skins that were at Quebec, and the other was to bring three months of supplies to the fort. The supplies were to last until a further ship arrived later that year under the command of Isaac de Razilly of the Company of New France.

Not long after, some natives in a canoe advised de Caën that Quebec had been taken by the English. Being skeptical, de Caën sent two Frenchmen who had been in the pinnace with Boullé and some natives to Quebec to find out if this was true.

They arrived in Quebec at night and surreptitiously learned that the English did indeed have control of the fort. Instead of returning post-haste to de Caën with this news, they went to Guillaume Couillard's home.

Couillard asked them why they had come. They replied that de Caën had sent them to see if the fort had been captured, at which Couillard exploded:

> Alas, what simpletons and ill-advised men you are. Can't you see that it is?

He told them that they had no sense and that the natives would let the English know that they were present. He added that their presence required him to report this matter to Captain Lewis Kirke.

If he did not do so, not only would his life be at stake, but his whole family would be endangered. He then took the two Frenchmen to Kirke, who detained them and put them to work.

The English did not immediately return to England with their French prisoners. They only left on their return trip to Europe a few months later.

Chapter Reference Sources

- *Backwoodswoman, The* by Isabel Skelton, chapter I.
- *Canadian Frontier, 1534-1760, The* by W. J. Eccles, p. 32-33.
- *Canadian Types of the Old Regime: 1608-1698* by Professor Charles W. Colby, p. 131-33; 137.
- *Champlain - Founder of Quebec, Father of New France* by N. E. Dionne, ch. X.
- Champlain, Samuel de" by Marcel Trudel in the *Dictionary of Canadian Biography*, Vol. 1. p. 195-96.
- *Champlain: the Life of Fortitude* by Morris Bishop, ch. XIX.
- *Documents Relating to The Seigniorial Tenure in Canada* edited by William Bennett Munro, p. xxiv.
- *First Establishment of the Faith in New France* by Father Christian Le Clercq, p. 296; 305.
- *History of the Canadian People, A* by M. H. Long, Vol. I, p. 127.
- *Jesuit Relations*, Father Charles Lalemant, Vol. IV, p. 256-58 and note 21.

- *Jesuit Relations*, Father Paul Le Jeune, Vol. V, p. 276-77 and note 11.
- *Louis Hébert - Premier Colon Canadien et sa Famille* by Abbé Azarie Couillard Després, ch. VIII; p. 84-85.
- *Samuel de Champlain - Father of New France* by Samuel Eliot Morison, p. 190-98; 200-02.
- *Works of Samuel de Champlain, The* general editor H. P. Biggar, Vol. V, p. 270-72; 298-99; and Vol. VI, p. 48; 53; 56; 62-63; 68; 82; 92-94; 108-11; 122-23.

Chapter XVI

HÉBERT FAMILY STAYS - CHAMPLAIN LEAVES

After the English took over the fort they raised their own flag, and the passing days seemed like months to Champlain. He was no longer happy being in Quebec now that he was no longer in charge. He asked Lewis Kirke to allow him to leave Quebec and go to Tadoussac to wait there until the English ships sailed for England. Kirke agreed.

Champlain boarded a flyboat, under the command of Thomas Kirke, with his possessions and the two native girls Hope and Charity. The boat departed on July 24, 1629. En route to Tadoussac they encountered a ship commanded by Emery de Caën.

Cannon shots were exchanged and de Caën loudly cried out "Quarter! Quarter!" He did so to indicate that he wanted mercy. Combat then ceased. Kirke told Champlain to speak to de Caën stating that if the other vessel fired upon them ".... you will die. Tell them to surrender." Champlain replied that he had no authority over them. However he did speak to Emery de Caën whose men then laid down their arms.

At Tadoussac, "General" David Kirke spoke to Champlain about Hope and Charity. The French turncoat Nicolas Marsolet had written a letter to Kirke stating that a council of Indian chiefs was opposed to these young native girls going to France.

It was at this time that David Kirke told Champlain that he would not allow him to take Hope and Charity to France. This was so notwithstanding that Champlain had proposed to give to the natives a gift of beaver skins belonging to him of a value of 1,000 livres in exchange for his taking the girls to France.

According to Champlain the girls were grief stricken since they considered Champlain as a father to them because he fed and clothed them. Since the girls could not go to France, they asked Champlain to arrange for them to stay in Quebec with Guillemette Couillard (Louis Hébert and Marie Rollet's daughter).

Champlain wrote that he asked Guillaume Couillard (Guillemette's husband) to place the girls with his wife for as long as they wished to stay there. Couillard said to Champlain that they would be looked after as if they were his own children for as long as they wished to stay.

Several months after Champlain arrived at Tadoussac, David Kirke's vessel sailed for England carrying Champlain, the people from the fort who were not remaining there, and the Catholic priests. The ship arrived at Plymouth on October 20, 1629 and remained there for five days. It reached Dover on October 27th prior to the French party being transported to France.

However, Champlain as well as David Kirke had learned at Plymouth that some six months earlier (on April 29, 1629) France and England had declared peace between their two countries. This meant that the capture by the Kirkes of Quebec (which had occurred in July 1629) was illegal.

Rather than returning to France with his compatriots, Champlain decided to travel to London to see the French Ambassador, Monsieur de Chateauneuf. He wanted the Ambassador to advise the King of England of events that had happened with a view to having Quebec restored to France by the English.

To get to London he first traveled to Gravesend on David Kirke's ship. From there Kirke chartered a boat for their trip down the Thames River to London. It arrived on October 29, 1629.

Champlain was able to travel about freely in London. He met with the French Ambassador and reported to him on events in New France. He remained in London until early December and then returned to France.

Prior to Champlain's departure, the Ambassador told him that the King of England and His Council had promised to return New France to the French King.

However no indication was given of when this might occur.

Pontgravé had returned to France in 1629 with the party from New France. In addition to de Monts, Pontgravé is another person who deserves greater recognition for the role that he played in the history of Canada. He was born at St. Malo, France about 1554. He first came to New France before 1600 to trade in furs. In 1600 he again arrived in the St. Lawrence as the second-in-command of the expedition to Tadoussac by Pierre Chauvin.

Pontgravé was in charge of the 1603 voyage to the same area. This trip had been organized by the Governor of Dieppe, Aymar de Chaste. On this venture Samuel Champlain was on board as an observer. Consequently Pontgravé and Champlain developed a friendship that lasted over 25 years.

Pontgravé was also at St. Croix in 1604 with the de Monts expedition that included Louis Hébert and, as a cartographer, Samuel Champlain. In 1605 Pontgravé was the deputy of de Monts at Port Royal.

Pontgravé's function was primarily that of a trader, not an explorer or settler. He was again in the St. Lawrence area in 1608 and was wounded at Tadoussac by Basques who were illegally trading in furs. He continually returned to the St. Lawrence River area for many summers. On many occasions he wintered there until the Kirkes captured the fort in 1629.

In fact in 1619 the merchants, stirred up by Boyer, purported to place Pontgravé in charge of Quebec rather than Champlain who was then in France. Of course Champlain did not tolerate his ouster. In 1620, with his wife Hélène, he returned to Quebec bearing a vice-regal commission giving him authority there.

Champlain, who was then about fifty-two years old, wrote of this incident that, while he and Pontgravé were friends and he respected him as a father, he would not allow him to be given "what belonged to me by right or reason." He added that they "had lived as good friends in the past, and I desired to so continue."

Champlain presented a letter from the King entitled "Dearly beloved". This letter gave Champlain command over exploration and colonization. However it clearly indicated the mindset of those in authority in France when the letter also stated that the exploration and colonization was not to:

.... disturb or hinder your factors, clerks and agents in the matter of the fur trade in any manner and fashion whatsoever.

Pontgravé worked for Guillaume de Caën for most of the 1620s. The natives liked Pontgravé. Sagard wrote that he was "a good old man, naturally jovial", drank plentifully, and screamed for help from the pain of his gout. He had a booming voice and a personality to match it.

He was sick, afflicted with gout, bed-ridden and in his seventies when the Kirke brothers captured Quebec in 1629. He was transported to England, then to France in that year, after which he disappears from the history books. Champlain made no mention of his old friend in his work entitled *Voyages* of 1632.

As the Champlain biographer Samuel Morison wrote, Pontgravé was:

.... one of the most important founders of Canada ....

When the English had taken control of Quebec in July 1629, Marie Rollet (the widow of Louis Hébert) and Guillaume and Guillemette Couillard (her son-in-law and daughter) were devastated. They expected to be unceremoniously ejected from their homes and their farms and to be shipped back to France. They anticipated that the life that they had built in New France would be destroyed.

The prospect of returning to France was not as daunting to Champlain. In the 27 years after his initial arrival in Quebec, Champlain resided in Paris a majority of the winters and occasionally entire years.

In contrast Louis Hébert, Marie Rollet and the Couillards never returned to France after they had immigrated to Quebec. From that time on each of them lived their lives continuously in their adopted homeland. None of them had a desire to return to France.

If they returned to France Marie, Guillaume and Guillemette would have no home, lands or livelihood. As for Champlain's situation, the French-Canadian historian N. E. Dionne wrote that in 1622 Champlain had been granted "the privilege of trading for 11 years...."

Another biographer Samuel Morison wrote that Champlain "had accumulated a goodly sum from the fur trade". However, the Hébert family had been prohibited from dabbling in the fur trade. If they returned to France they would have little funds to resettle there. Indeed their future looked bleak.

To their surprise and joy Lewis Kirke, the Commander of the Quebec fort, treated them in a gracious and generous manner. Kirke was a well-mannered man of about 30 years whose mother was French.

He invited them to remain in their homes and on their lands in Quebec. This conquering Englishman went further. He proposed far better terms for Marie Rollet and Guillaume Couillard to stay on and live in Quebec than the French fur-trading companies had ever permitted to Louis Hébert.

Kirke told them that they could reap their crops and deal with them as they wished. They were even free to trade their crops to the natives in exchange for furs. Kirke added that if they stayed in Quebec and found that circumstances under the English were not to their liking they would have the option to continue in Quebec or to return to France.

If they made the latter decision, he assured them that they would be conveyed to France the following year when the English vessels returned. He magnanimously added that if they elected to go back to France the following year they would be paid four livres for every marketable beaver skin that they had acquired.

Marie and the Couillards decided to consult Champlain about the proposal from Lewis Kirke. However, as will be seen, it was an offer that they could not refuse. Champlain later wrote:

> They asked my advice more out of seemly deference to my opinion than with any intention of following the advice I might give.

He stated that he decided to give them advice that would not leave them destitute. He told them that the matter of greatest importance was their exercise of the Roman Catholic religion, and that there was no possibility of this happening in Quebec under the Protestant Englishmen. The English would not permit the Jesuits or the Recollets to stay in New France.

He added rather gratuitously, since they were all devout practicing Catholics and knew the facts well, that the Holy Sacraments would be unavailable while the English were in control. He wrote that he then suggested they stay for the year, reap their grain, sell their furs, and in the following year abandon their lands and return to France when the English vessels returned.

He never recommended that they should consider the terms of the beneficial proposal made by Lewis Kirke to be a blessing to them. After all they had been settled in Quebec for many years and had enthusiastically adopted it as their homeland. He did not recommend that they stay forever in the place where Louis Hébert had died and was buried and where the Couillards' children and Louis Hébert and Marie Rollet's grandchildren had all been born.

An early Canadian historian, the Jesuit Priest François du Creux, writing in 1664 stated that Champlain:

> .... mourned the lot of the Hébert family, whose choice it had been to remain in the midst of a wicked and perverse generation rather than return to France.

According to Champlain, Marie Rollet and the Couillards told him that they would follow his advice. They never did, choosing to remain in their adopted homeland for the rest of their lives.

In fact, the Couillards presented another granddaughter to Marie Rollet during the English occupation of Quebec. Elizabeth Couillard was born at Quebec on February 9, 1631. An interesting aspect was that at Elizabeth's baptism Lewis Kirke was the godfather.

It was not only the families of Marie Rollet and the Couillards who chose to stay in Quebec. So too did Pierre Desportes, Nicolas Pivert, Abraham Martin, Guillaume Hubou and their respective families. As Le Clercq wrote:

> Those who chose to remain in the country obtained some advantage, especially the family of Monsieur Hébert.

Collectively it was these six families that remained in Quebec that kept alive the flickering flame of the French presence there during the English occupation. These families were quite close and socialized with each other.

For example Pierre Desportes' daughter Hélène married Guillaume, the only son of Louis Hébert and Marie Rollet. As noted elsewhere in this book Marie Rollet had married Guillaume Hubou two months prior to the conquest of Quebec. The date of the marriage was May 16, 1629.

Abraham Martin was called "l'Ecossais [the Scot]" because he was born in Scotland. He had come to Quebec in 1613 as a ship's pilot for the fur-trading company. In 1635 he acquired 32 acres of land on the heights of Quebec.

After he cleared his land it became known as the Plains of Abraham. In 1759 this was the site of the decisive battle in which the British troops of General James Wolfe defeated the French forces led by the Marquis de Montcalm. Both Wolfe and Montcalm were killed, but the battle later resulted in British control of Canada with the signing of the 1763 Treaty of Paris. This Treaty ended the

Seven Years War that in the North American phase was called the French and Indian War.

Because of his influence on events in Canada in 1628 and 1629, it is fitting to mention some further information concerning David Kirke, a fascinating person in his own right.

As noted previously, it was only when he returned to England in October 1629 that David Kirke found out that his conquest of Quebec three months earlier had been illegal. France and England had declared an armistice in the spring of that year. Kirke was not happy on learning that England was negotiating to return New France to its former enemy. He had incurred heavy expenses in his ventures in New France and, being a privateer, had expected to reap the rewards of his victory.

David was born in France. His father Jarvis Kirke (also called Gervase) was an English gentleman who had resided in Dieppe for many years. While he was living in France he had married a French woman Elizabeth Goudon of Dieppe. This meant that David Kirke and his brothers were half-French. Jarvis later returned to England with his family and became a prosperous merchant in London.

David was a member of the English Merchant Adventurers to Canada and was in his early thirties when he commanded the expedition which conquered Quebec in July 1629. For his services he did not receive money, nor was he reimbursed for expenses which he and his associates paid for out of their own pockets.

However, the Kirkes did take commercial advantage of the three year delay by England in restoring New France to the French in 1632. David received a knighthood from King Charles I of England in 1633. As well, in November 1637, Charles I granted all of Newfoundland to a prominent group of Englishmen including Sir David Kirke and the Duke of Hamilton.

In that same year Kirke became the sole owner of Newfoundland and he was its Governor until the early 1650s. During his Governorship he encouraged immigration to Newfoundland and promoted development of its resources.

He was recalled to England in 1651 because of his failure to make tax payments to the Crown. He was subsequently imprisoned for seizing Ferryland, situated on the Avalon Peninsula. Cecil, Lord Baltimore, took control of Newfoundland in 1660.

Another matter of interest concerning David Kirke is that his daughter married Pierre Esprit Radisson, the great Canadian explorer and fur trader. Radisson is best known for his involvement with his brother-in-law Médard des Groseilliers in inducing Prince Rupert to enter into the fur trade in North America.

As a result of their meeting with Prince Rupert in England, the Prince persuaded his cousin King Charles II to grant the Charter dated May 2, 1670 that established the Hudson's Bay Company (HBC). The HBC is the oldest existing corporation in the world.

The controversial David Kirke has been considered a hero by some Englishmen and a pirate by some Frenchmen. He died in jail in England in 1654.

Chapter Reference Sources

- *Champlain: The Life of Fortitude* by Morris Bishop, p. 29-30; 110; 245; 276-77; 281-82.
- *Champlain - Founder of Quebec, Father of New France* by N. E. Dionne, p. 138; 199; 207.
- *First Establishment of the Faith in New France* by Father Christian Le Clercq, p. 304.
- "Gravé du Pont, François" by Marcel Trudel in the *Dictionary of Canadian Biography*, Vol. I. p. 345-46.
- *History of Canada or New France, The* by Fr. François du Creux, p. 56.
- *History of the Canadian People, A* by M. H. Long, p. 300.
- *Jesuit Relations* by Father Paul LeJeune, Vol. V, p. 276-77; note 11; note 13.
- "Kirke, Sir David" by James Marsh in the *Dictionary of Canadian Biography*, Vol. I. p. 404-07.
- *Louis Hébert - Premier Colon Canadien et sa Famille* by Abbé Azarie Couillard Després, p. 92.

- *Old Quebec - Trails and Homes* by E. C. Woodley, p. 16-17.
- *Samuel de Champlain - Father of New France* by Samuel Eliot Morison, p. 175-76; 189; 225.
- *Works of Samuel de Champlain* general editor H. P. Biggar Vol. IV, p. 363-65; Vol. V, p. 298-99; Vol. VI, p. 69-73; 77-78; 111-12; 123; 144-45; 150.

Chapter XVII
QUEBEC AND ACADIA RESTORED TO FRANCE

As discussed in the previous chapter, England and France had declared an armistice and ceased to be at war three months before the capture of Quebec. Champlain had only learned that the seizure was unlawful when he arrived with David Kirke in England in October 1629.

From that time on Champlain devoted a good deal of his efforts to having New France restored to France. The fur merchants, the fishing interests and the clergy of France also lobbied the French authorities with the same objective in mind.

Champlain wrote letters to King Louis XIII about the potential riches to be derived from the resources of New France. He confirmed his desire to find the elusive passage to the Orient. He added a request to the King that his personal allowance that he had received for the past 25 years be maintained.

The reacquisition of New France was not the most important matter on the King's agenda. Although negotiations were carried on, it was not until 1632 that the matter was resolved.

Charles I of England was spurred into action with respect to surrendering New France by his need for money. At the time Charles was having difficulties with a recalcitrant Parliament which had declined to vote subsidies to him in the previous four years. He was desperate for funds and came up with a proposal that met this need.

When Charles had married Louis XIII's sister, Henrietta Maria, the promised dowry of his wife was 800,000 crowns. However, only half of this amount had been paid. Charles agreed to restore New France, including Acadia, to the French upon payment to him of the outstanding balance of his wife's dowry.

This was agreed to and on March 29, 1632 a treaty was signed at Saint Germain-en-Laye providing for the return of

New France to the French. In effect, France reacquired these lands simply by discharging an overdue obligation.

The Company of One Hundred Associates, which had been given the monopoly by Cardinal Richilieu in 1627, was not then ready to dispatch an expedition to New France. Consequently in 1632 Louis XIII granted a one year monopoly to Emery de Caën. This former Huguenot had become a Catholic, perhaps to assist him in receiving royal favors.

De Caën readied an expedition to New France. Prior to its departure, Cardinal Richilieu had decided to confer on the Jesuits the sole spiritual authority in New France. He revoked the permission of the Recollets to evangelize or go there.

Consequently three Jesuits, Fathers Paul LeJeune and Anne de la Noüe and Brother Gilbert Buret accompanied the de Caën party when it set out from France in the spring of 1632. So too did a few dozen settlers, but not Champlain.

Champlain had been in France continuously since the late autumn of 1629 and, among other matters, was engaged in writing his 1632 *Voyages*. He dedicated this work to Cardinal Richilieu.

An interesting aspect is that in these writings, Champlain expunged a number of references to the Recollets which had appeared in his 1619 *Voyages*. This included the first journey of the Recollets to New France. In the 1632 work Champlain lauded the Jesuits, but praiseworthy comments about the Recollets had disappeared.

Although his writings were voluminous, Champlain divulged little of significance relating to his personal life. For example, there is no reference to his marriage to Hélène Boullé.

De Caën arrived at Quebec on July 5, 1632. He met with Thomas Kirke explaining the developments that had occurred. He advised him of the signing of the Treaty of

Saint Germain-en-Laye and called upon him to surrender the fort.

Kirke, loyal to Charles I, agreed to do so conditional on his seeing the original Commissions and Letters Patent from the Kings of England and France. These were produced for him on the following day. They ordered that the fort be surrendered within eight days.

Kirke did surrender the fort on the eighth day and de Caën then assumed possession in the name of the King of France. The English Cross of St. George was lowered and the French fleur-de-lis flag was raised at the fort on July 13, 1632. The inhabitants who had remained at Quebec were overjoyed when they saw the flags on the masts of the French ships and realized that their motherland had reacquired New France.

De Caën and Fathers LeJeune and de Noüe ascended the precipitous pathway to the heights and saw some ramshackle buildings. Further on they sighted the stone home built by the Héberts. It had been well cared for and was in fine shape and sat amidst vegetable gardens.

In the *Jesuit Relations*, Father LeJeune wrote that after de Caën, he and the others had arrived in Quebec:

> We celebrated Holy Mass in the oldest home in this country, that is the home of Madame Hébert [Marie Rollet] who had dwelled close by the fort during her husband's lifetime.... This is the only French family settled in Canada....

Father Le Jeune added that the Hébert family had been endeavoring to find a way to go back to France before the de Caën expedition arrived. It may be that LeJeune was told this more to indicate to him that they had remained loyal to France and had missed the opportunity to practice their faith. Pursuant to Kirke's promise Marie Rollet and her family could have returned to France, but decided not do so and instead remained in New France during its possession by the English.

Father LeJeune wrote that at the first Mass in Marie Rollet's home after his arrival, everyone sang the *Te Deum* with overflowing hearts. This is a Christian hymn commencing *Te Deum laudamus* [We Praise Thee O God].

Abbé Després quoted a Monsieur Bourassa (probably Henri Bourassa founder of the Montreal newspaper *Le Devoir*):

.... under the roof of the widow Hébert when she sang the *Te Deum* and offered to God her sacrifice of thanksgivings, there was no other thought but to remain in Canada, and certainly one would be unable to find another more deserving of an equal honor.

All was not sweetness and light once de Caën and the others arrived in 1632. The English had been trading alcohol for furs with the natives.

While under the influence of the unscrupulous white man's firewater the natives had engaged in murderous quarrels. Father LeJeune wrote that since he had arrived he had seen only intoxicated natives shouting and raving day and night; they fought and wounded each other; and killed Madame Hébert's cattle.

LeJeune added that when the natives sobered up, they blamed the white man saying:

If you had not given us brandy or wine, we would not have done it... it is not we who did that, but you who gave us this drink.

Once the English left New France the sale of alcohol to the natives was forbidden. Any breach of this prohibition would result not only in the transgressors license to trade being cancelled, but also in his being flogged with a cat-o'-nine tails.

LeJeune later wrote that notwithstanding this restriction, the natives secretly obtained alcohol from time to time. Members of the tribe of a native who had been imprisoned for murdering a Frenchman told LeJeune that it was the brandy that had committed the murder, not the prisoner who had been intoxicated at the time. The natives told him:

Place your wine and your brandy in jail; it is your drinks that cause all the trouble, and not us.

In the fall of 1632 de Caën's ships sailed back to France, although he remained in New France until his royal grant expired.   After the arrival of the ships in France the Company of One Hundred Associates, to which Champlain belonged, was up-dated as to the conditions existing in New France and de Caën's profitable fur-trading there that season.

Spurred by Cardinal Richilieu, that winter the Company organized for its new venture in New France. It made arrangements for outfitting an expedition. On March 23, 1633 three vessels of the Company left Dieppe for New France.

One of them carried Champlain on his last voyage there.   There were some 200 people in the expedition including Fathers Jean de Brébeuf and Ennemond Massé but only three females.

On the journey across the Atlantic Ocean the ships ran into bad weather, storms and fog.   They only reached Quebec on May 23, 1633, exactly two months after their departure.

Cardinal Richilieu had designated the now 66 year old Champlain as his lieutenant in New France and commander of the expedition.   For the first time Champlain was put in complete command of the St. Lawrence, but he was never commissioned as the Governor of New France.

His arrival after an absence of some three and one-half years was heralded by a cannon-shot.   Father LeJeune hastened to the fort to welcome the group.   There he saw a troop of French soldiers bearing muskets and pikes and beating drums.   De Caën had previously relinquished the keys of the fort so that they could be handed over to its new commander, Champlain.

The natives were delighted at the return of Champlain with his party.   According to LeJeune eighteen canoe-loads of natives descended on Quebec. In a speech welcoming Champlain, one of their leaders told him:

.... when the French were absent the earth was no longer the earth, the river was no longer the river, the sky was no longer the sky.

LeJeune echoed thoughts similar to those expressed by Louis Hébert on his deathbed, when he wrote:

Those who think that the savages have dull and heavy intellects will recognize by this speech that they are not so stupid as they have been painted.

The French term "sauvage [savage]" was used in this context (as it was by Louis Hébert) to denote one who is uncivilized or a member of a primitive tribe, and not in the sense of a barbarian or a wild person.

Although he had first come to the New World some 30 years before and spent most summers and some winters there, Champlain never did learn a native language. Consequently in addressing the natives the day after his arrival, he did so through an interpreter.

On this occasion the interpreter for Champlain was Olivier Letardif. In his speech Champlain recounted his friendly activities and that of the French towards them. He proclaimed that the French had always loved the natives. Champlain, perhaps presciently anticipating the beginnings of a Metis people in Canada, told them:

When that great house shall be built, then our young men will marry your daughters.

However, Champlain's forecast in his speech that then "we shall be one people" was wide of the mark.

Champlain immediately set to work to reconstruct the fort and its various buildings. He also advanced the fur trade. In 1634 he had a fort built at Trois Rivières that developed into an important trading post.

To fulfill a vow that he made if Quebec was returned to France, in 1633 Champlain undertook the construction of a chapel near the fort. It was completed that fall and High Mass was celebrated in it every Sunday.

Champlain dedicated the chapel to the Blessed Virgin Mary and it was named Notre Dame de la Recouverance [Our Lady of the Recovery]. This was in thanksgiving for the return of New France to the French.

Champlain was disappointed that Hope and Charity, the young girls gifted to him by the natives, had during the English occupation left the Couillards and returned to their own tribe. Nothing more was heard of them.

In his advanced years, Champlain seems to have become a more devout Catholic, perhaps anticipating that he had not long to live. He asked Father LeJeune to be his personal confessor.

A religious milieu sprang up around the fort due in no small part to the influence of the Jesuits. During meals the separated and childless Champlain had Jesuits and others as guests. However, there was little chitchat during the meals; rather there was reading aloud of the history and lives of Catholic saints. LeJeune wrote that Champlain was:

.... a chief so zealous for the glory of our Lord and for the welfare.... [of the Frenchmen].

The community soon witnessed a steady and frequent occurrence of Masses, confessions and prayers. The atmosphere was in sharp contrast to the "eat, drink and be merry" banquets of "The Order of Good Cheer" that Champlain and Louis Hébert enjoyed in Acadia during the winter of 1606-07.

After Champlain's return to Quebec in 1633 liquor was banned, the inhabitants were no longer rowdy, and the atmosphere at the fort was more serene. At the request of Marie Rollet the school that she had established for the French and native children was carried on by the Jesuits in their chapel, which had more space than her home.

Champlain seemed reinvigorated after his return to Quebec. He had rebuilt the fort, constructed a chapel, impressed the natives, encouraged the missionaries, and promoted the fur trade.

True his wife Hélène was thousands of miles away in France, true his dream of finding the Northwest Passage was dashed, and true there were only about 12 dozen settlers in Quebec at the time. Nevertheless he was the man in charge, respected and honored.

But fate intervened. In October 1635 Champlain suffered a paralytic stroke and was permanently bedridden.

Unknown to Champlain, about this time the associates of the Company of New France were meeting in Paris at the request of Cardinal Richilieu in order to replace Champlain. The definitive reason for his dismissal is not known. The Company appointed as his successor Charles de Montmagny.

Happily for Champlain, a loyal Company man to his death, he never knew of this occurrence. He never recovered from his stroke and died on Christmas day 1635. One of the giants of Canadian history had passed on.

Champlain had made his last will and testament from his sick-room bed on November 17, 1635. Prior to that, while in Paris during the English occupation of Quebec, he had bestowed on his wife Hélène everything that he possessed in France. Consequently in his final will of 1635 he left her only his papers and a few other items.

Champlain dedicated most of his remaining assets to the Blessed Virgin Mary. He did this by means of bequests to the Jesuit missions in Quebec; to Notre Dame de la Recouverance (the Quebec chapel he had built and named in honor of the Blessed Virgin Mary on his return to New France in 1633); and for masses to be said for the repose of his soul.

He left a long list of monetary and other bequests to other religious groups and to a number of settlers. For example, he bequeathed:

- 300 livres to Marguerite Couillard, the granddaughter of Louis Hébert and Marie Rollet;

- the same amount to Hélène Desportes, the wife of Guillaume Hébert, the only son of Louis and Marie; and

- to Marie Rollet a pair of white fustian "brassières". Today this French word means baby vests or short straps, but at the time it likely denoted bodices. Presumably they were clothes that Champlain's wife Hélène had not taken with her when she returned to Paris some eleven years earlier.

Champlain's testamentary generosity did not go without a hitch. His cousin Marie Hersaut (nee Camaret) challenged the will as residuary legatee. A favorable ruling resulted in Champlain's cousin, and not the chapel of Notre Dame de la Recouverance, receiving his shares in the Company of One Hundred Associates.

Champlain's biographer, Morris Bishop, wrote that:

 In France, Champlain was soon forgotten.

It was not until the latter half of the 1800s, over two hundred years after his death, that people in Canada started referring to him as the "Father of New France". This belated recognition may have been due in part to the publication in 1870 of six volumes of Champlain's works that had been prepared in French by Abbé C. H. Laverdière.

Champlain's name became more prominent when a group of Toronto businessmen formed an organization in 1905 that they named The Champlain Society. The major purpose of this Society was to publish manuscripts and new editions relating to Canadian history. During the period 1922-36, a main publication of the Society was the bilingual edition in six volumes of Champlain's works.

Chapter Reference Sources

- *Champlain: The Life of Fortitude* by Morris Bishop, p. 283-86; 289-91; 299-301.
- "Champlain, Samuel de" by Marcel Trudel in the *Dictionary of Canadian Biography*", Vol. 1. p. 195-98.

- *Jesuit Relations* by Father Charles Lalemant, Vol. IV, p. 257-58; note 21.
- *Jesuit Relations* by Father Paul LeJeune, Vol. V, p. 41; 43; 49-51; 201; 203; 211; 231.
- *Louis Hébert - Premier Colon Canadien et sa Famille* by Abbé Azarie Couillard Després, p. 97.
- *Pioneers of France in the New World* by Francis Parkman, Vol. Two, p. 246; 272; 276-79.
- *Samuel de Champlain - Father of New France* by Samuel Eliot Morison, p. 198; Chapter XIV.
- *Three Centuries of Canadian Story* by J. E. Wetherell, p. 120-121.
- *White and the Gold - the French Regime in Canada, The* by Thomas B. Costain, p. 121-23.

Chapter XVIII

MARIE ROLLET'S CONTRIBUTIONS TO CANADA

Marie Rollet, the Couillards and the small contingent of French settlers who had remained in Quebec when the English conquered it in 1629 were undoubtedly filled with joy with the return of the French in 1632.

As mentioned in a prior chapter, a couple of months before the surrender of Quebec in 1629 the widowed Marie Rollet married for a second time. Her new spouse was Guillaume Hubou. Not much is known about Hubou, although the author Isabel Skelton states that he was of Norman blood and an honorable man.

It is interesting to note that in the *Jesuit Relations*, Father LeJeune wrote that on his return and that of the French to Quebec in 1632 Mass was celebrated "in the home of Madame Hébert", not in that of Madame Hubou. LeJeune subsequently referred to "Madame Hébert" in his writings on more than one occasion; in doing so he never mentioned the name Marie Hubou.

It is not surprising that Hubou was from Normandy. Normans were the largest number of colonists in New France during the first two-thirds of the 17th century. For example Jean Nicolet, who married Marie Rollet and Louis Hébert's granddaughter Marguerite Couillard, came from Normandy.

The second principal area from which colonists came to New France was from the west-central district of Perche in France. This was primarily due to the efforts of Robert Giffard (a surgeon who had come from Perche and had been granted a seigneury in New France in 1634). Giffard, who came to Canada sometime after the Hébert family, was a medical doctor. In her book, Maude Abbott wrote:

> Had it not been for the tenacity of purpose and agricultural intelligence of Louis Hébert, surgeon-apothecary of Paris, and the sagacious forethought and public-spirited citizenship of Robert Giffard, a physician of Normandy [sic] in making good their habitation and success here, the little colony of Quebec could hardly

have withstood the storms and difficulties that beset it, and the advance of civilization in this locality might have been for many decades deferred.

After the arrival of the Jesuits in 1632, Marie Rollet was instrumental in the establishment of a school for the children of the community as well as for the native children. Due to her charitable and caring nature, a number of native children were brought up and clothed and schooled by her in her home.

As others joined these beginners, it soon became apparent that a more suitable site was needed to accommodate her increased number of students. Accordingly, the chapel of the Jesuits was adapted for this purpose. Both French and native youths were educated there, including the children of Pierre Desportes, Abraham Martin, and the Couillards.

The girls, native and French, were placed on one side of the chapel while the boys were on the other side. Instruction included the "A, B, Cs", but was preceded by prayers and catechism. In the *Jesuit Relations* Father LeJeune wrote that the natives:

.... think they are doing you some great favour in giving you their children to instruct, to feed and to dress.

This condescending approach of LeJeune to the native children is in stark contrast to the congenial attitude of Louis Hébert to the natives during his lifetime. Hébert's sentiments must have been shared by Marie Rollet for it was she who included the native children in the school that she established.

One of the children whom the Jesuits taught lived with Marie Rollet or the Couillards. He was neither French nor native Canadian. He was a native boy from Madagascar.

He was brought to Quebec in 1628 by the English and, according to Father LeJeune, sold by the Kirkes to a person named le Bailly. His new owner in turn gave him to the "estimable family that is settled here" i.e. Marie Rollet and the Couillards.

This boy was apparently given the name Olivier LeJeune. There are a couple of amusing stories concerning this youngster.

In one incident Father LeJeune, addressing him in French, asked him if there were "Mosquées [Mosques]" in Madagascar. The lad told him that there were, just like those in Quebec that he saw the French and the English shoot with. The Jesuit priest smiled at this response, realizing that the boy had mistaken a Mosque for a "mousquet [musket]".

On another occasion this dark skinned boy from Madagascar was asked by his "mistress" (either Marie Rollet or Guillemette Couillard) if he wanted to be baptized as a Christian "and be like us". He asked if this meant he would be skinned saying:

> You say that by baptism I shall be like you. I am black and you are white. I must have my skin taken off then in order to be like you.

All present laughed heartily at these remarks, as did the boy on being told of his misunderstanding. He was baptized not long after.

This youngster was a slave when he was brought to Quebec, the first slave in recorded Canadian history. It is a little known fact that black slavery existed in Canada for over two centuries.

An article appeared in the 2003 issue of *The Beaver* magazine that recounted the history of slavery in Canada. On August 1, 1834 the *Slavery Abolition Act* was passed by the British Parliament. This Act was applicable to all of Great Britain's colonies. When it came into effect it ended Canada's sordid history of slavery.

Marie Rollet continued to live her praiseworthy life in Quebec with her second husband, Guillaume Hubou. Her daughter Guillemette and son-in-law Guillaume Couillard continued to present her with grandchildren, a total of ten by 1648. Marie Rollet died in Quebec in 1649, the year after her grandchild Gertrude was born.

In her book *The Backwoodswoman* Isabel Skelton wrote of the "admirable" Marie Rollet:

.... she, and she alone, has to speak to us today for the countless hundreds of silent French-Canadian frontierswomen who shared with their husbands the hardships and dangers of the early life, and at the same time brought up those large families of sons and daughters that have ever been the pride of their nation.... She was a thrifty, provident, hospitable matron, an excellent manager of her house and her resources. She was ambitious and a woman of strong character, but just and kind and deeply devoted to her Church and religion.

Professor Charles W. Colby wrote of Marie Rollet:

Madame Hébert, whose personal virtues have already been mentioned, was as good a colonist as her husband. Her attachment to Canada was tested in 1629 when the English captured Quebec. Neither she nor any of her family went back to France. The Héberts had taken root and become Canadians.

In 1928 Leon Ville authored a book in French dedicated to the life of Marie Rollet. This is a creative work that may, perhaps, appeal to young people. It contains many inventive conversations of Marie Rollet, Louis Hébert and the Couillards. It also contains a number of fanciful drawings.

During her lifetime Marie Rollet was the distaff side of a remarkable duo in Canadian history. The ventures of Marie and her husband Louis Hébert saw them share:

- the hardships and dangers of traveling to and living in the frontier;

- tragedies and triumphs;

- courage and vision;

- trials and tribulations;

- sadness and joy; and

- the distinction of being the first permanent colonial settlers in Canada.

Together they conquered the virgin forest and built a home for their family. They planted a garden and crops and sustained themselves from the land. They ministered to the sick and the needy.

In addition, Marie Rollet played a very significant role in founding the first formal school in Canada. It can be said that her initiative in this respect was the initial groundwork leading to the eventual formation of Canada's educational system.

Marie was the venerable pre-eminent forerunner of a remarkable group of Canadian women. By virtue of her trail-blazing pioneer efforts and her numerous Canadian progeny over the centuries and today, Marie Rollet richly and singularly merits the accolade "Mother of Canada".

Chapter Reference Sources

- *Backwoodswoman, The* by Isabel Skelton, p. 32-33.
- *Canadian Types of the Old Regime; 1608-1698* by Professor Charles W. Colby, p. 131; 150.
- *History of Medicine in the Province of Quebec* by Maude Abbott, p. 14.
- "In Bondage" by Tom Derreck in the *The Beaver* magazine February/March 2003, p. 14-19.
- *Jesuit Relations* by Father Paul LeJeune, Vol. V, p. 63-65; 197-199.
- *Louis Hébert - Premier Colon Canadien et sa Famille* by Abbé Azarie Couillard Després, p. 102-04.
- *Marie Rollet - Les Premieres Colons Franco-Canadiens* by Léon Ville, *passim*.
- *Samuel de Champlain - Father of New France* by Samuel Eliot Morison, p. 221.

SECTION D

THE FAMILY AND EXTENDED FAMILY

OF LOUIS HÉBERT AND MARIE ROLLET

Marie Rollet et Ses Enfants

Daughters Anne and Guillemette, and son Guillaume.

Monument in Montmorency Park, Old Quebec City, Quebec.
Sculptor - Alfred Laliberté.

Guillaume Couillard

Monument in Montmorency Park, Old Quebec City, Quebec
Sculptor - Alfred Laliberté.

Chapter XIX

GUILLAUME COUILLARD AND GUILLEMETTE HÉBERT - A PIONEERING CANADIAN COUPLE

Guillaume Couillard and Guillemette Hébert were both emigrants from France who made their permanent home in Canada in the early 1600s. It was in Quebec where they were married, where all of their children were born and where they lived the rest of their lives after their arrival. They never returned to the country of their birth.

Various facts and anecdotes involving this historic duo are interspersed throughout this book. The following recaps or adds to a number of highlights of their pioneering lives.

It is through Guillaume, Guillemette and their children that the lineage of Canada's first permanent colonial settlers, Louis Hébert and Marie Rollet, has continued and proliferated throughout Canada.

Guillaume Couillard was born in France about 1591, likely in St. Malo. He came to New France in 1613 as an employee with the fur-trading company at Quebec.

When he arrived he was a carpenter, a sailor, and a caulker. According to Champlain, Guillaume was a "good sailor, carpenter and caulker".

The French word for sailor is "matelot". It is interesting to note that matelot was the name of Champlain's dog. As well, the original grant of land to Louis Hébert was named the "Sault-au-Matelot".

Couillard had been at the fort in Quebec for four years when the Hébert family, including Guillemette, settled there in 1617. As time went by he became attracted to Guillemette, fell in love with her, and married her on August 26, 1621.

In due course Couillard became a farmer, working alongside his father-in-law. He cleared additional lands and, upon Louis Hébert's death in 1627, he and Guillemette inherited half of Hébert's estate.

Couillard farmed the lands that he and his wife inherited together with the land that he had previously cleared. He was a self-sufficient farmer, who also had livestock on their farm.

Couillard was the initiator of an historic event in Canadian agriculture on April 27, 1628. On that day he used a plow on his land, the first person to use this implement in Canada.

As has been previously noted, the provident Couillard and the widow Hébert (Marie Rollet) would provide food grown on their lands to the inhabitants of the fort. This was particularly necessary when the fort's supplies were meager due to failure of the arrival of the supply ships from France.

In addition to being a successful farmer, he also worked at the fort when needed. However, Couillard had a mind of his own.

This is illustrated by the incident in 1628, previously mentioned, in which he stood up to Champlain and refused to undertake a hazardous trip to Tadoussac to repair a pinnace there. This was so notwithstanding Champlain's attempt to intimidate Couillard by threatening to incarcerate him if he refused to go.

Couillard was not being cowardly in his decision. He may have thought Champlain's plan was foolhardy. However, it is likely that his overriding concern was that if he was killed he would leave his children with no father and his wife a widow.

Champlain wrote of Couillard that:

.... during the fifteen years he has been in the service of the Company he had always shown himself courageous in everything he did...

Champlain added that Couillard

.... could only be called upon in case of necessity.

Nevertheless, Couillard did demonstrate his customary willingness to help the fort (of which he was no longer an employee). He offered to caulk two boats that were at the fort, rather than the pinnace at Tadoussac.

Couillard and his family showed their bravery in 1629 when they and his mother-in-law, Marie Rollet, elected to remain in Quebec when the English conquered it. He and Guillemette displayed their charity in agreeing to take into their home and care for the adolescent native girls, Hope and Charity. This occurred after David Kirke refused Champlain's request to take the girls to France with him.

In the 1630s Couillard acquired additional lands and established a flour mill. He was appointed in 1639 by Charles Huault de Montmagny, the Governor of New France, to be the inspector of the crops and food of the Quebec inhabitants. In addition, in the early 1640s the Company of New France commissioned him to make lime for it.

Couillard had become quite prosperous due to his hard work, prudence and entrepreneurial skills. In 1652 he and his wife Guillemette made a grant of land to the clergy in Quebec in order that a church could be built on it. This is the land on which the Basilica of Quebec City was subsequently built.

The Couillards were given a small gift in return for these lands - a church pew in perpetuity for them and their descendants. The authors endeavored to ascertain the present status with respect to the family pew, but never received a reply to their enquiry.

Jean de Lauson became the Governor of New France in 1651. Although his main objective was to make as much money as he could for himself and his family from the fur trade, he was instrumental in Couillard being appointed a nobleman in 1654.

This was in recognition of the services which Couillard had rendered to the colony. He was now Charles Guillaume Couillard de Lespinay. The original name of his father-in-law Louis Hébert's seigneury had been Lespinay.

Couillard selected as his motto "God aided the first colonist". His coat of arms was:

Azure, a dove with golden wings spread out, holding in its beak the branch of a green olive tree.

Guillaume and Guillemette also gave land to the nuns of L'Hôtel-Dieu, a hospital. This grant, made in 1661, was to be used as a cemetery to bury impoverished patients who died in the hospital.

On March 4, 1663 Guillaume Couillard, then in his 70s, passed away. He had:

- arrived in Quebec as a young employee of the fort;
- progressed to being a successful and well-off farmer, landowner and businessman; and
- been ennobled by the King of France.

Guillaume was, as Champlain wrote, a courageous man who had:

.... gained the friendship of everyone, so that people all did what they could for him.

Couillard's statue forms an integral part of a magnificent monument in the heart of old Quebec City. This statue commemorates in bronze Couillard's ground-breaking first use of the plow in Canada, and his historic contributions to the country he loved.

Louis Hébert, Marie Rollet and their children also form part of this creative monument, which shows Guillemette as a child. Guillemette was born in France about 1606 and came to Canada with her parents and siblings in 1617.

She married Guillaume Couillard in 1621 when she was approximately 15 years old. When they were married, Guillaume was almost twice her age.

After the English took control of Quebec in 1629, Guillemette stayed in Quebec with her husband and children as well as with her mother Marie Rollet.

Guillemette and Guillaume were quite prolific; in all they had 10 children. It is through this pioneering couple and their children that numerous Canadians trace their ancestry to Guillemette's illustrious parents Louis Hébert and Marie Rollet.

Guillemette and Guillaume suffered through some sad incidents involving several of their children.   Their daughter Louise died only four years after her marriage to Olivier Letardif in 1637.   Two sons of the Couillards, Nicolas and Guillaume Jr., were killed by the Iroquois in 1661 and 1662 respectively. However, their hearts were gladdened by the birth of grandchildren from time to time.

Guillemette was a friend to the native children. This is evidenced by her unhesitating willingness to take Hope and Charity into the Couillard home in 1629. It should be noted that it was these native girls who asked to be sent to the Couillards when David Kirke refused to let Champlain take them to France after the fall of Quebec.

In addition Olivier LeJeune, the boy from Madagascar, was also welcomed into their home by Guillemette and Guillaume. With these extra children, together with their own children and servants, the Couillard homestead must have been a continual beehive of activity.

Guillemette was a faithful and benevolent Catholic. The grants of land by her and Guillaume have already been noted.   Three years after Guillaume's death she sold the lands and house of the Sault-au-Matelot to Bishop François Laval in order that a Quebec seminary could be constructed thereon.

The sale contract was dated April 10, 1666.   The purchase price was 8,000 livres, which was paid by installments. A seminary sits on these lands today in the heart of Old Quebec City.

A number of Guillemette's offspring were upset by the sale of the fief Sault-au-Matelot. Some of them sued and court proceedings were carried on for generations.

In 1679, some 16 years after her husband's death, Guillemette enlarged the 1661 grant that she and Guillaume had given to the nuns of L'Hôtel-Dieu.

Towards the latter part of her life Guillemette retired to the L'Hôtel-Dieu Convent. A few years before her death, her father Louis Hébert (who had died over 50 years earlier) was re-buried in the Recollet chapel. Likely unable to walk to the chapel for the ceremony, Guillemette was carried there to witness the move. This was indicated by Father Le Clercq, who was present for the event.

In 1683 Guillemette made her last will and testament. Among her bequests were grants to the nuns, the Recollets and other religious institutions.

Guillemette died on October 19, 1684. She was then in her late seventies. She was laid to rest in the chapel of L'Hôtel-Dieu next to her husband Guillaume Couillard.

This remarkable woman left a legacy of being one of Canada's first permanent settlers, a loving wife and mother, a generous benefactor, a gracious and devout human being and, with her husband Guillaume, a progenitor of numerous Canadians.

Chapter Reference Sources

- *Champlain: The Life of Fortitude* by Morris Bishop, p. 250; 281.
- "Couillard de Lespinay, Guillaume" by Honorius Provost in the *"Dictionary of Canadian Biography"*, Vol. I, p. 236-37.
- *First Establishment of the Faith in New France* by Father Christian Le Clercq, p. 281.
- "Hébert, Guillemette" by Ethel M. G. Bennett in the *"Dictionary of Canadian Biography"*, Vol. I, p. 366-67.
- "Hébert, Louis" by Ethel M. G. Bennett in the *"Dictionary of Canadian Biography"*, Vol. I, p. 367-68.
- *Louis Hébert - Premier Colon Canadien et sa Famille* by Abbé Azarie Couillard Després, p. 64-65; 74-76; 82; 97; 104-05; ch. XIII; ch, XIV.
- *Works of Samuel de Champlain, The* general editor H. P. Biggar, Vol. V, p. 270-72.

Chapter XX

PROMINENT SONS-IN-LAW OF THE COUILLARDS

Guillemette and her husband Guillaume Couillard, the daughter and son-in-law of Louis Hébert and Marie Rollet, contributed greatly to the fledgling community of Quebec. Louise, Marguerite and Elizabeth (three of the Couillard daughters) married men who in their own right became prominent within the community. These men were Olivier Letardif, Jean Nicolet and Jean Guyon Jr.

As noted earlier in this book, the interpreter on the occasion of Champlain's speech to the natives on his triumphal return to New France in 1633 was Olivier Letardif.

Interpreters were essential at that time in New France. They were needed to assist both Champlain and the French fur-traders in dealing with the natives. They also aided the missionaries in this respect in their attempts to convert the natives.

Two of the young Frenchmen who lived among the natives in order to become proficient in their tongue and capable interpreters were Olivier Letardif and Jean Nicolet.

Letardif was an interesting personality. He was born at Honfleur in France about 1604 and came to Quebec as a 17 year old. He was one of the signatories to the petition of August 18, 1621 to King Louis XIII complaining about the abuses of the merchant Company. Letardif learned to speak and interpret several native languages including Huron, Montagnais and Algonquin.

When the Kirkes took Quebec in 1629, he was working there as a clerk and a sub-agent of the Company of New France. It was he who at that time surrendered the Habitation keys to Lewis Kirke. In this respect Champlain wrote of Letardif:

> He acquitted himself of the duty like a man of character, the said du Pont [Pontgravé] the Agent in Chief being in bed at the time, suffering from the gout and unable to act.

Champlain also wrote that Olivier was skilled in the languages of the natives and accustomed to trading with them. He also noted that he was very suitable for doing so.

Letardif returned to France in 1629 after the defeat of Quebec, but came back with the de Caën party to Quebec after it was restored by the English to the French in 1632. Thereafter he continued to act as an interpreter when needed. In 1633 he was appointed chief clerk of the Company of New France. He later became its general manager.

In addition he took part in missionary activities. He even baptized an Indian child, acted as a godfather of another, and adopted a third. The adopted native child, Marie Manitouabewick, subsequently married Martin Provost. This 1644 marriage was the first formalized wedding in Canada of a French man and a native woman.

On November 3, 1637 Letardif married Louise Couillard, not then 13 years old. Louise, born in Quebec, was the oldest child of Guillaume and Guillemette Couillard.

On May 23, 1637, Letardif and his future brother-in-law Jean Nicolet had become co-owners of a commoner's grant of 160 acres near Quebec, called the Belleborne fief.

Nine years later Olivier became a seigneur of part of Beaupré and subsequently became the General and Special Procurator of the Company of Beaupré. Letardif later acquired land and settled at Château Richer. He died there in 1665. His first wife Louise had predeceased him only four years after their marriage.

Jean Nicolet married Marguerite Couillard on October 22, 1637 only a couple of weeks before Letardif married her sister Louise. Marguerite was not yet a teenager.

Nicolet was born in Cherbourg in Normandy in 1598. He came to Canada in the service of the fur-trading company when he was 20 years old. Shortly after his arrival, Champlain sent Nicolet to live among the Algonquin tribe on Allumette Island.

He spent two years there, becoming initiated into the Algonquin lifestyle and customs. He mastered both their language and that of the Hurons. Nicolet's acceptance by the Algonquins was such that he was invited to speak at their assemblies. He was also asked to go with them to negotiate peace with the Iroquois, a delicate mission which he successfully fulfilled.

In 1620 he returned to Quebec on completion of his assignment among the Algonquins and reported on his activities. He subsequently lived for a time with the Nipissings at Nipissing Lake in north-east central Ontario. He participated in the fur trade with the natives on behalf of the merchant Company.

When Quebec surrendered to the English in 1629, Nicolet did not return to France with Champlain. Instead he took sanctuary among the Hurons.

When the French resumed possession of New France in 1632, Nicolet reappeared at Quebec. A short time later he was sent by the Company of New France to parley with the Winnebagoes in the Green Bay area of present-day Wisconsin.

The intent was to pacify relations between these natives and the native trading partners of his employer. He brought with him a small group of Hurons and succeeded in his mission.

He took advantage of his trip to do some exploration in the area, the first white man known to do so. He even searched, without success, for the elusive passage to the Orient.

Nicolet returned to Quebec in 1635, settling at Trois Rivières. It was two years later that he and his future brother-in-law, Olivier Letardif, became co-owners of the Belleborne fief.

In 1642 while en route to Trois Rivières, Nicolet drowned when the shallop he was traveling in capsized. Although he did not have a lengthy life, his work amongst the natives and his explorations were significant for this time.

Another early French immigrant to Canada with a connection through marriage to the Hébert family was Jean Guyon Sr. of Montagne, Perche. He came to Beauport in Quebec in 1634 with Robert Giffard who granted him a fief close to the Buisson River. He then added the noble surname "du Buisson" to his name.

His son, Jean, was born in France in 1619 and came to Canada with his father in 1634 or perhaps a year or so later. On November 27, 1645 at Quebec the younger Jean married Elizabeth Couillard, a granddaughter of Marie Rollet and Louis Hébert. Two violinists played at the wedding ceremony, something unprecedented in Canada.

The younger Jean Guyon was also known as Jean Guyon du Buisson. He became a surveyor, and was the first person to acquire that skill in Canada. In the 1660s he was known as the "King's surveyor" in Quebec.

Jean Guyon spent the latter part of his life at Château-Richer near Beauport and the St. Lawrence River. He died there on January 13, 1694. His wife Elizabeth died on April 5, 1704.

In some cases the name "Guyon" became "Dion" at a later date. A number of descendants of Jean and Elizabeth today bear the name Dion including apparently Celine Dion, the internationally-renowned singer from Quebec.

Jean and Elizabeth Guyon had 12 children. On February 19, 1692 two years prior to Jean Guyon's death, Marie Madeleine Guyon (their 18 year-old granddaughter) married Antoine Goulet at L'Ange-Gardien, Quebec.

Antoine had been born at Château-Richer, Quebec in August of 1666. He was the son of Jacques Goulet and Marguerite Mulier, who had been born in France and later immigrated to New France.

A number of the descendants of Antoine Goulet and Marie Madeleine Guyon entered the fur trade. Some were engaged by the North West Company and others by the

Hudson's Bay Company.   These companies were the principal fur traders in Canada in the late 1700s and well into the 1800s.

Many of the descendants of Louis Hébert, Marie Rollet and the Couillards played prominent roles in the history of Western Canada. For example Elzear Goulet was involved with the Red River Settlement and in the Red River Resistance led by Louis Riel in 1869-70. This Resistance led to the formation of the Province of Manitoba in 1870.

Chapter Reference Sources

- "Guyon du Buisson, Jean (junior)" by Honorius Provost *Dictionary of Canadian Biography* , Vol. I, p. 359-60; 366.
- *History of the Canadian People, A* by M. H. Long, Vol. 1, p. 82-83.
- *Jesuit Relations* by Father Paul Le Jeune, Vol. V, p. 287-88, note 49.
- "Letardif, Olivier" by Marcel Trudel in the *Dictionary of Canadian Biography* Vol. I, p. 473.
- *Louis Hébert - Premier Colon Canadien et sa Famille* by Abbé Azarie Couillard Després, ch. XII.
- "Nicollet [sic] de Belleborne, Jean" by Jean Hamelin in the *Dictionary of Canadian Biography* Vol. I, p. 516-18.

Chapter XXI

THEIR LEGACY LIVES ON

The distinguished lives of Louis Hébert and Marie Rollet enriched many facets of early Canadian history. Various descriptive words about them spring to mind when one reflects on their accomplishments as permanent settlers in Canada some 400 years ago. They include trailblazers, settlers, pioneers, visionaries, and the list goes on and on. Their actions showed their courage and optimism.

Louis Hébert's love for Canada was nurtured over four centuries ago when he lived in Acadia. While there, his influence in the colony was recognized by his occasionally serving as its acting governor. As indicated in the book *Great Moments in Pharmacy*, Bear River and Bear Island (which are near Annapolis Royal, Nova Scotia) are:

.... contractions of "Hébert Island" and "Hébert River" – the names by which they were first designated.

During his time in Port Royal, Louis Hébert saw first-hand the beauty and the abundance of the land. He was smitten by its alluring charms.

When he and Marie returned to Paris in 1613, they shared their vision of the "brave New World" with their children. As a result, this pioneer family left Paris in 1617 for a new life thousands of kilometers westward across the Atlantic Ocean to a new home on the Quebec frontier.

The Hébert family did so notwithstanding most inauspicious, unfriendly and dictatorial conditions imposed on them at Honfleur, their French port of departure. En route to their destination they were confronted by another unfeeling antagonist, the hazardous elements of nature. The ill winds, the harsh storms, the mountainous swells, and the looming icebergs filled their crossing with dread and threatened a fatal disaster for all.

The combination of unsympathetic Company officials and menacing weather may have sorely tested the wisdom of their decision to leave their family and friends to venture to an unknown destiny in a land far away. However if they may have momentarily had second thoughts about their momentous relocation, these quickly vanished when they reached their destination.

The following list sets forth many of the pioneering achievements of Louis Hébert and Marie Rollet.

- They were the first colonial family to permanently settle in Canada.

- They were the first immigrants to build a permanent home for their family and live in it for the rest of their lives.

- They were the first pioneers to clear the land, cultivate the soil, and establish a permanent farm.

- Louis Hébert was the first settler to practice his profession as an apothecary/pharmacist in Canada, and likely in North America, and to act as a physician.

- Louis Hébert was the first European botanist to permanently live in Canada.

- Louis Hébert was the first individual to obtain title to his land in Canada.

- Louis Hébert was the first person to be appointed a nobleman and King's Procurator in Canada.

- Marie Rollet was the first woman from France to cultivate the Canadian soil.

- Marie Rollet was the first permanent colonial homemaker in Canada with her own home.

- Marie Rollet established the first school in Canada for native and community children.

The lands that Louis Hébert obtained title to were granted by the Duke of Montmorency on February 4, 1623. Today this property is in the heart of Old Quebec City and contains such sites as Notre Dame de Quebec (the Roman Catholic Basilica Cathedral), the Quebec Seminary, the

Museum of French America, and streets named for Louis Hébert and his son-in-law Guillaume Couillard.

The Parish of Notre Dame is the oldest one in North America outside of Mexico. Over the past 350 years the Catholic Church at this site has developed into a beautiful Basilica that is situated in Quebec City at 20 rue Buade. It is a magnificent structure with stained-glass windows, episcopal throne dais, sculptures, paintings, canopy, and a chancel lamp that was donated by Louis XIV.

At one time Laval University was on these lands, but in 1946 it moved to the western end of Quebec City. The Hotel Marie Rollet at 81 rue Sainte Anne is very close to the Basilica. This is a small *pension* in the European tradition that was named after Louis Hébert's wife.

In Park Montmorency, which is close to the Basilica, is the monument to Louis Hébert, his wife Marie Rollet, their children and their son-in-law Guillaume Couillard.

The remarkable couple, Louis Hébert and Marie Rollet, shared many traits. They had an enlightened and loving attitude towards the natives. They considered them intelligent human beings, lacking only formal education and sophisticated ways.

They were both courageous. As noted earlier, on one occasion Louis Hébert rushed to aid his compatriots who were being attacked by natives. As for Marie Rollet, she remained in Canada amidst the British conquerors when most of her compatriots had returned to France.

Louis, Marie and their family were venturers who pioneered permanent settlement by Europeans in Canada. Louis Hébert made his memorable mark in New France by being the first European to establish a permanent home and farm for his family in Canada.

He also led the way as a pioneer in inaugurating the practice of a professional apothecary in Canada and, perhaps, in the entire Western Hemisphere. He was a pioneer pharmacist who came to live in the New World. Further, he augmented and enhanced his professional expertise by consulting with the local natives. From them he learned their medicine, the medicinal and curative herbs they used, and their folklore.

Hébert's legacy as a "pharmaceutical pioneer" with an "intrepid spirit of self-sacrifice and service to fellowmen" lives on today as evidenced by those words from the book *Great Moments in Pharmacy*.

On August 2, 1930, a large number of pharmacists from all parts of Canada gathered at Annapolis Royal prior to the Annual Meeting of their national association [Canadian Pharmacists Association], to honor Louis Hébert. The ceremony was sponsored by the Nova Scotia Pharmaceutical Society to memorialize his contributions to their profession. A plaque in acknowledgement of Hébert's status as the pioneer apothecary in Canada was unveiled at this commemoration. It reads as follows:

> **To honour the memory of Louis Hébert pioneer Apothecary in Acadia 1604 this Tablet is placed here by the Nova Scotia Pharmaceutical Society A.D. 1930.**

Additional recognition of Louis Hébert's contribution to his profession has been made by Ordre des Pharmaciens du Quebec (Pharmacists Association of Quebec). This Asssociation grants an annual award called the Prix Louis Hébert to an outstanding pharmacist in the Province of Quebec.

Hébert's professional legacy is furthered affirmed by the fact that on September 11, 1985 a pharmaceutical company sent to all Canadian pharmacists a special limited edition of a stamp (produced by the government of Canada) portraying Louis Hébert. This stamp was issued to coincide with the 45th International Congress of Pharmaceutical Sciences. The cover letter that was sent to all Canadian pharmacists stated that:

> .... this stamp commemorating pharmacists around the world .... will be treasured by many as a collector's item.

The lives of Guillemette Hébert and Guillaume Couillard (the daughter and son-in-law of Louis Hébert and

Marie Rollet), add to the luster of this quintessential pioneer family. It is through them that the blood of Louis Hébert and Marie Rollet has flowed and to this day continues to flow through the veins of numerous Canadians across this great country.

Louis Hébert was a noble man not only by royal designation, but more so in his character. As Isabel Skelton in writing of the pending death of Marie Rollet wrote of both of them:

> Her day drew to its close, but not so the way of life she and her husband established. This backwoods settler class which they so excellently typify came to be the backbone of our nation.

A 19th century historian E. Salone is quoted by Charles W. Colby as summing up Louis Hébert's career as follows:

> And so this Parisian chemist became not only the first Acadian and the first Canadian, but the first seigneur of New France.

Professor Colby's own words commemorating Louis Hébert (which may also be applied to Marie Rollet) deserve to be preserved:

> Hébert's labours are so meritorious that posterity should preserve with pious care whatever is known about him.

Their stirring legacies are sinews that bind Canada's historic colonial past to the prodigious modern day nation that it has become. As Canada's premier pioneers and for their outstanding contributions, Louis Hébert and Marie Rollet are truly giants in Canadian history.

Chapter Reference Sources

- *Great Moments in Pharmacy* by George A. Bender, p. 72-75.
- *The Backwoodswoman* by Isabel Skelton, chapter p. 32-33.
- *Canadian Types of the Old Regime: 1608-1698* by Professor Charles W. Colby, p. 127; 130.
- *Louis Hébert - Premier Colon Canadien et sa Famille* by Abbé Azarie Couillard Després, *passim*.

Appendix "A"
TITLE TO THE FIEFS OF LOUIS HÈBERT

The following is the authors' translation of the French text found in the Appendix to the book titled *Louis Hébert - Premier Colon Canadien et sa Famille* by Abbé Azarie Couillard Després.

Henri de Levis, Duke of Ventadour, peer of France, Lieutenant General of His Most Christian Majesty of the Government of the Province of Languedoc and Viceroy of New France.

To Whom it may concern, Greetings:

Let it be known that Louis Hébert, one of the subjects and inhabitants of the aforesaid country of New France, has pointed out that for many years he continuously endured long and difficult labors and dangers and expended efforts in clearing lands in Canada, and that he is the head of the first family which has lived there since the early 1600s up to the present, and to which he brought them with all their goods and means he had in Paris, having left his parents and his friends in order to devote himself to the commencement of a colony and a Christian people in these places in which they are without the knowledge of God in order that they might be imbued with His Holy Light; for which the said Hébert settled on the edge of the great St. Lawrence River, at the site of Quebec close to the Habitation which was erected by a company authorized by His Majesty and confirmed by us; that he has by his own work and industry, assisted by his domestic servants, cleared certain portions of the land in an enclosure, and constructed accommodation for himself, his family and his livestock; which lands, accommodation and enclosure he had obtained from Monsieur the Duke of Montmorency, our predecessor as Viceroy, as a gift and grant in perpetuity by letters issued on Saturday February 4, 1623; We for the considerations cited herein and to encourage those who hereafter desire to live and dwell in the said country of Canada, have given, ratified and confirmed, do give, ratify and confirm, to the said Louis Hébert and his successors and heirs and pursuant to the authority granted to us by His Majesty all the said arable lands cultivated and comprised in the enclosure of the said Hébert including also the house and buildings comprised therein at the said site of Quebec on the great St. Lawrence River to be enjoyed as a noble fief by him and his heirs and having caused so to happen and by his personal and loyal acquisition to fully and peacefully dispose thereof as he may so wish, all relevant to the fort and chateau of Quebec with the responsibilities and conditions which hereafter are imposed on him by us, and for the same considerations have made a gift to the said Hébert and to his successors, inheritors and heirs extending to a French league of land situated near the said Quebec on the St. Charles River which is limited and bounded by the Sirs de Champlain and de Caën in order to possess, clear, cultivate and inhabit and in the same way to be considered to be under the same conditions as the first grant giving very express directions and prohibitions to all persons of such position and rank that they are not to be troubled or prevented from the possession and enjoyment of these lands, houses and enclosure, enjoining Sir de Champlain our Lieutenant General in New France to support the said Hébert towards all and against all in his aforesaid possession and enjoyment. For such is our wish.

Given at Paris this last day of February 1626.

(Signed) DE VENTADOUR.

And more below

By my said Lord Viceroy

GIRARDET.

Sealed with red wax

173

Appendix "B"

PLAQUE IN PARIS HONORING LOUIS HÈBERT

**Current Photo of the plaque on the house
where Louis Hébert was born.**

129 rue Saint-Honoré, Paris, France.

Mortier d'Or [Golden Mortar]
Recent photo of Louis Hébert's Paris home.

129 rue Saint-Honoré, Paris, France.

Appendix "C"

MAPS OF INTEREST RE: LOUIS HÈBERT

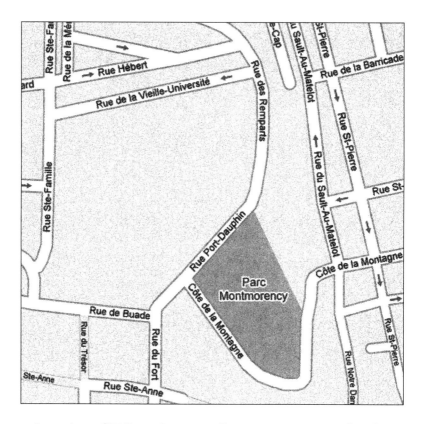

Location of Hébert Street and Montmorency Park - the site of the Monument to Louis Hébert, Marie Rollet with her children, and Guillaume Couillard.

Current Map of Old Quebec City, Quebec.

Location of Hébert [Bear] River
Map of Port Royal
by Marc Lescarbot circa 1606

BIBLIOGRAPHY

In the preparation of this book numerous materials, both primary and secondary, were reviewed and assessed. The following is a selection of some of the more pertinent references.

Abbott, Maude, *History of Medicine in the Province of Quebec*, (McGill University, Montreal, 1931).

Barber, Katherine, Editor in Chief, of *The Canadian Oxford Dictionary*, (Oxford University Press. Toronto, 1998)

Bender, George A., *Great Moments in Pharmacy* (Parke, Davis & Company, Detroit, 1966).

Bennett, Ethel M. G., (1) "Hébert, Louis" in *Dictionary of Canadian Biography* (University of Toronto Press, 1966) Vol. I.
(2) "Hébert, Guillemette", in *Dictionary of Canadian Biography*, (University of Toronto Press, 1966) Vol. I.
(3) "Rollet, Marie", in *Dictionary of Canadian Biography*, (University of Toronto Press, 1966) Vol. I.

Biard, Father Pierre, *Jesuit Relations*, translation, edited by Reuben Gold Thwaites (The Burrows Brothers, Cleveland, 1898), Vol. III.

Biggar, H.P. (1) *The Early Trading Companies of New France* (University of Toronto Library, 1901).
(2) *The Works of Samuel de Champlain*, translation general editor, (Champlain Society, Toronto, 1922-1936) Vol. IV; Vol. V; and Vol. VI.

Bishop, Morris, *Champlain: The Life of Fortitude*, (McClelland and Stewart Limited, Toronto, 1963).

Brown, George W., *Building the Canadian Nation - 1492-1849*, (MacFadden Books, New York, 1968).

Champlain, Samuel, *The Works of Samuel de Champlain*, translation general editor H. P. Biggar, (Champlain Society, Toronto, 1922-1936) Vol. IV; Vol. V; and Vol. VI.

Charlton, M., "Louis Hébert" in the *Johns Hopkins Hospital Bulletin* (Johns Hopkins Hospital, 1914), Vol. 25.

Colby, Charles W., (1) *Canadian Types of the Old Regime: 1608-1698*, (Henry Holt & Co., New York, 1908).
(2) *The Founder of New France: a Chronicle of Champlain*, (Glasgow, Brook, Toronto, 1915).

Conan, Laure, *Louis Hébert - Premier Colon du Canada*, (Imprimerie de L'Événement, 1912).

Costain, Thomas B., *The White and the Gold - the French Regime in Canada*, (Doubleday and Company, Garden City, New York, 1954).

Creux, Fr. François du, *The History of Canada or New France* (The Champlain Society, Toronto, 1951).

Derreck, Tom, "In Bondage", in *The Beaver* magazine (Canada's National History Society, Toronto, February/March 2003).

Després, Abbé Azarie Couillard (1) *La Première Famille Française au Canada* (L'École Catholique des Sourds- Muets, Montreal, 1906).
(2) *Louis Hébert - Premier Colon Canadien et sa Famille* (Desclée de Brouwer & Cie, Paris, 1913). [Translation by George and Terry Goulet.]

Dionne, N. E., *Champlain - Founder of Quebec, Father of New France*, (University of Toronto Press, Toronto, 1963).

Dumas, G. M.,"Le Clercq, Chrestien [Christian]" in the *Dictionary of Canadian Biography*, Vol. 1, (University of Toronto Press, Toronto, 1966) p. 438-41.

Eccles, W. J., *The Canadian Frontier, 1534-1760*, (University of New Mexico Press, Albuquerque, 1974).

Encyclopedia Britannica, (Encyclopedia Britannica, London, (1994-2002) Vol. 9 and 12.

Fortier, L. M., *Champlain's Order of Good Cheer*, (Thomas Nelson & Sons Ltd., Toronto, 1928).

Hamelin, Jean "Nicollet de Belleborne, Jean" in the *Dictionary of Canadian Biography,* (University of Toronto Press, 1966), Vol. I.

Hattie, W. H. "On Apothecaries, Including Louis Hebert" in *The Canadian Medical Association Journal*, January 1931.

Hreinsson, Viðar *Icelandic Sagas - The Complete Sagas of Iceland*, editor, (Leifur Eiriksson Publishing, Reykjavik, 1997), Vol. V.

Hunter, Douglas, "The Mystery of Champlain's Astrolabe" in *The Beaver* Magazine (Canada's National History Society, December 2004/January 2005).

Jarvis, Julia, *Louis Hébert* (Ryerson Press, Toronto, 1928).

Jefferys, C. W., *The Picture Gallery of Canadian History*, (The Ryerson Press, Toronto, 1942), Vol. 1.

Jenkins, Phil, "Field of Opportunity" in the *Canadian Geographic* magazine issue of March/April 1999.

Johnston, Jean, *Wilderness Women - Canada's forgotten history*, (Peter Martin Associates, Toronto, 1973).

Jurgens M., "Recherches sur Louis Hébert et sa famille" in *Mémoires de la Société Génealoquie Canadienne-Française*, Vol. VIII-No. 1, January, 1957; Vol. VIII-No. 3 July, 1957.

Kirbyson, Ronald C., *In Search of Canada*, (Prentice-Hall of Canada, Scarborough, 1977).

Lalemant, Father Charles, *Jesuit Relations*, translation edited by Reuben Gold Thwaites (The Burrows Brothers, Cleveland, 1898), Vol. IV.

Leacock, Stephen, *Canada - The Foundation of its Future*, (privately printed, Montreal, 1941).

Le Clercq, Father Christian [Chrestien], *First Establishment of the Faith in New France*, translation by John G. Shea, (John G. Shea, New York, 1881).

LeJeune, Father Paul, *Jesuit Relations*, translation edited by Reuben Gold Thwaites (The Burrows Brothers, Cleveland, 1898), Vol. V.

Lescarbot, Marc, *Nova Francia - A Description of Acadia, 1606*, translation by P. Erondelle, (George Routledge & Sons, London, 1928).

Long, M. H., *A History of the Canadian People*, (The Ryerson Press, Toronto, 1942), Vol. 1.

Marsh, James H., (1) "Kirke, Sir David" in the *Dictionary of Canadian Biography*, (University of Toronto Press, Toronto, 1966) Vol. I.
(2) *The Canadian Encyclopedia*, editor in chief (McClelland & Stewart Inc., Toronto, 1999).

Morison, Samuel Eliot, *Samuel de Champlain - Father of New France*, (Little Brown and Company, Boston, 1972).

Morton, W. L., *The Kingdom of Canada*, 2nd edition (McClelland and Stewart, Toronto, 1969).

Munro, William Bennett, editor *Documents Relating to The Seigniorial Tenure in Canada*, (Champlain Society, Toronto, 1908).

Parkman, Francis, *Pioneers of France in the New World*, (George N. Morang & Company, Toronto, 1900), Vol. Two.

Provost, Honorius, (1) "Couillard de Lespinay, Guillaume" in the *Dictionary of Canadian Biography*, (University of Toronto Press, 1966), Vol. I.
(2) "Guyon du Buisson, Jean (junior)" in the *Dictionary of Canadian Biography*, (University of Toronto Press, 1966) Vol. I.

Ryder, Hula, "Biencourt de Poutrincourt et de Saint Just, Jean de" in the *Dictionary of Canadian Biography*, Vol. 1.

Ryerson, Stanley B., *The Founding of Canada - Beginnings to 1815*, (Progress Books, Toronto, 1975).

Sagard, Brother Gabriel, (1) *Histoire du Canada*, (Chez Claude Sonnius, Paris, repr. 1994, c. 1636).
(2) *The Long Journey to the Country of the Hurons*, translation by H. H. Langton (The Champlain Society, Toronto, 1939).

Skelton, Isabel, *The Backwoodswoman*, (Ryerson Press, Toronto, 1940).

Sutherland J. C., *The Romance of Quebec*, (W. J. Gage & Co., Limited, Toronto, 1934).

Tanguay, Abbé Cyprien, *Dictionnaire Généalogique des Familles Canadiennes*, (Genealogical Publishing Co., Baltimore, 1967).

Thwaites, R. G. English translation editor *Jesuit Relations*, (Cleveland, 1896-1901) Multiple Volumes.

Tracy, Frank Basil, *The Tercentenary History of Canada - From Champlain to Laurier*, (P. F. Collier & Son, New York, 1908), Vol. I.

Trudel, Marcel (1) *The Beginnings of New France: 1524-1663*, translation by Patricia Claxton, (McClelland and Stewart Limited, Toronto, 1973).
(2) "Champlain, Samuel de" in the *Dictionary of Canadian Biography*, (University of Toronto Press, Toronto, 1966) Vol. I.

(3) "Gravé du Pont, François" in *The Dictionary of Canadian Biography*, (University of Toronto Press, Toronto, 1966) Vol.I.

(4) *Histoire de la Nouvelle France*, (Fides, Montreal, 1966), Vol. II.

(5) "In Search of Asia" in *Horizon Canada*, (Centre for the Study of Teaching Canada, Laval University, Quebec, 1987), Vol. 1.

(6) "Letardif, Olivier" in the *Dictionary of Canadian Biography* (University of Toronto Press, 1966), Vol. I.

Ville, Leon, *Les Premiers Colons Franco-Canadiens - Marie Rollet*, (Imprimerie R. Bussière 1928).

Wetherell, J. E., *Three Centuries of Canadian Story*, (The Musson Book Company Ltd., Toronto, 1920).

Woodley, E. C., *Old Quebec - Trails and Homes*, (Ryerson Press, Toronto, 1946).

Newspaper Articles and Television Productions

Calgary Herald - Newspaper, July 20, 2003.

Origins, A History of Canada- segments of this television documentary series, Havelock Gradidge, supervising editor, [History Television, Toronto].

The Globe and Mail Newspaper, November 30, 2002.

National Post Newspaper, July 29, 2000.

INDEX

OTHER LITERARY WORKS BY THE AUTHORS

GEORGE GOULET, B.A; LL.B; LL.M & TERRY GOULET, B.Sc (H.Ec)

The Metis – Memorable Events and Memorable Personalities, by George & Terry Goulet (FabJob Inc., Calgary, Alberta, 2006) - www.fabjob.com/metis.html.

The Trial of Louis Riel - Justice and Mercy Denied, by George R. D. Goulet, Principal Research Associate Terry Goulet (Tellwell Publishing, Calgary, Alberta, 1st ed., 1999); (FabJob Ltd., Calgary, Alberta, 2nd ed., 2001); (FabJob Ltd., Calgary, Alberta, 3rd ed. 2005) - www.fabjob.com/riel.htm.

On Eagles Wings, by George and Terry Goulet (FabJob Ltd., Calgary, Alberta, 2004).

Prostate Cancer -Treatment and Healing, by George and Terry Goulet, (FabJob Ltd., Calgary, Alberta, 2004).

"**The Role of Grandparents**", *Birth Issues,* by Terry and George Goulet (ASAC & CAPSAC, Calgary, Alberta, Spring 1997).

Public Share Offerings and Stock Exchange Listings in Canada, by George R. D. Goulet, Principal Research Associate Terry Goulet, (CCH Canadian Ltd., Toronto, Ontario 1994).

A Comparative Analysis of Constitutional Aspects of Securities Regulations in Canada and Australia, by George R. D. Goulet (Thesis for Master of Laws Degree, University of Toronto, 1990).

"**Overview of Canadian Securities Laws with Respect to Oil and Gas Financing**", by George R. D. Goulet, *Canadian-American Law Journal*, Vol. One (Gonzaga University School of Law, Spokane, Washington, Spring, 1982).

Dominus Vobiscum